Give ear, O my people, to my teaching;

incline your ears to the words of my mouth! . . .

We will not hide them . . . ,

but tell to the coming generation

the glorious deeds of the LORD, and His might,

and the wonders that He has done.

Psalm 78:1, 4

A DEVOTIONAL COMPANION

Blessings
&PRAYERS
FOR PARENTS

by Lisa M. Clark

CONCORDIA PUBLISHING HOUSE · SAINT LOUIS

This book is dedicated to my parents and in-laws, who are wonderful examples of loving Christian parents; my children, who daily teach me new lessons in parenting; and my husband, who is my partner and support as we learn and lead together.

TABLE OF CONTENTS

❖
PREFACE

$\mathcal{I}$ hope you're not disappointed, but this is not a how-to book. It is not a parenting guide in five easy steps or a miraculous family management plan.

Nor is it a comprehensive book. There is no way to encompass every parenting situation possible in an entire collection of books, much less in a small devotional such as this.

As a fellow parent, I'm keenly aware that my own experiences fall drastically short of equipping me to address all parenting questions with any sense of authority. So instead, I turn to my Father. Our Father. He knows better than any of us what it is to be a parent, and He provides comfort to His children through His Word.

As parents, caregivers, and those who support children in various ways, we are blessed to have a God who cares about each one of us and the families we have. He knows what it is to feel love, joy, pain, and all the emotions that come with caring for another.

And He invites us to spend time with Him in prayer and in His Word to be strengthened in the parenting roles we have. Whether you read this alone or with others, I pray that this book can be a useful tool as you learn more about your Father and His will for you. I pray that it can provide comfort and healing and encouragement as you experience both the pleasures and pains of caring for God's children.

Your Sister in Christ,

Lisa

A MODEL
FOR DAILY PRAYER

Let my prayer be counted as
incense before You, and the lifting
up of my hands as the evening
sacrifice!   *Psalm 141:2*

*A*s parents and those who support children, we benefit in exercising our spiritual lives on a daily basis so that we may better serve our families with joy. Jesus Himself took time out of His demanding ministry to pray to His Father. God invites us to spend time with Him as well, and He promises to hear our prayers.

Following, you will find a suggested format for prayer time, whether you do this by yourself, with your spouse, or with a group of other parents. This book provides a section for each devotional component in this format. The table of contents will help guide and focus your meditation.

Invocation: In the name of the Father and of the Son and of the Holy Spirit. Amen.

Devotional reading: Each devotion deals with a topic pertaining to parenting. Note that there are five main themes: joy, sorrow, fear, stress, and peace in parenting. Also, devotions focused on different stages of parenting are present in each theme. Take a moment to find a devotion that is particularly meaningful for you or your audience today. At the end of each devotion, you will find a suggestion for some of the following parts to your daily prayer.

Scripture reading: Our heavenly Father addresses us as His children, and He gives comfort, direction, and love to us, the parents of His next generation. Take time to read

© iStockphoto.com

some of these words to you from Your loving God.

Prayer: General Prayers are provided for common times or needs throughout your week. For a more particular theme or issue, look at the Topical Prayers section to assist your time with the Lord. Don't forget, of course, that heartfelt prayers written by you are precious to your Father. There is space throughout this book to jot down thoughts, prayer requests, and the like.

Hymn: Hymns can provide a powerful response to God's love and a meaningful way to express our needs. Whether you sing these or read them as poems, these hymns can provide added depth to your devotional time. One hymn, "Loving Father, Guide Your Children," is original to this book and applies to the concerns and joys of Christian parenting.

Meditations

Make me to know Your ways, O Lord; teach me Your paths. Lead me in Your truth and teach me, for You are the God of my salvation; for You I wait all the day long.

Psalm 25:4–5

JOY IN PARENTING

YOU ARE MINE

I have called you by name, you are
Mine.   *Isaiah 43:1*

I get it!

I remember telling myself this as I kissed my sobbing newborn son's forehead. I had given him only a handful of kisses, but I knew the love I had for him was unconditional in a way that I never before understood. Yes, I loved him and spoke to him and prayed for him long before I heard his cry. But when I held him in my arms, I remember praying to God: *Oh, I get it!*

Of course I have loved others before, but it usually came after I knew the person. I could trust him or her; I felt love in return. But my son had very little idea who I was. He didn't know what was happening to him in that hospital room, and he was showing his frustration at the whole ordeal. I knew that I loved him regardless of how he felt about me. I just *loved* him.

Those moments were such a tangible picture of how God loves me, how He loves all of us. Before we knew His name, even when we cried out in anger and confusion and sin at our sorry state, God loved us. We don't deserve it, and we more often look like the red-faced bawler than the sweet cherubic face we see on greeting cards. But God picked us up, washed us clean, and told us of the sweet comfort of His unconditional love.

My love for my children is flawed and tainted with my own sin. As much as I love them, I grow impatient with their needs. The joy I felt when I first saw their faces has been reduced to a halfhearted hug as I rush to the next task. At times, it's my own face that is reddened with anger and frustration and misunderstanding. But I know that my heavenly Father is perfect. His love is unconditional, and He forgives me when I am His disobedient child or my family's insufficient mother.

But now thus says the LORD,

He who created you, O Jacob,

He who formed you, O Israel:

"Fear not, for I have redeemed you;

I have called you by name, you are

Mine."   *Isaiah 43:1*

Maybe you felt the instant joy when you saw your child's face for the first time. Maybe you were confused yourself, not sure what to do with this little person. You may have been too sick or exhausted to know what was happening. But the joy we have in parenting is a gift from our God, and the joy He has for us is unconditional and without measure.

As you close this time of meditation, consider turning to the Hymns section of this book

© iStockphoto.com

to "Go, My Children, with My Blessing." Today, focus on stanza 1. Think about the words "You are My own." Consider also the words from the passage in Isaiah above: "you are Mine." Think of the joy God must have when He says this to us. Think of the joy these words give you as you know whose you are. Finally, think of ways to show this joy to your children so they know that they belong to you and to God.

ABBA

You have received the Spirit of adoption as sons, by whom we cry, "Abba! Father!"

Romans 8:15

𝓕acebook is full of his updates. Instagram knows his face. This little adopted boy is the pride and joy of his parents, and no one knew he was coming.

Well, that's clearly an exaggeration. Even though there were no belly photos or countdowns displayed, this dear child was hoped and prayed and sought for—long before he was home in the arms of his loving family. The excruciating wait and unanswered questions finally faded away as the joy of his parents was fulfilled.

Adoption is a beautiful picture of a parent's love—in many ways. First, there is the selfless love that led the birth mother and birth father to make the excruciating and sacrificial choice to place their child in the care of others. To carry a child throughout pregnancy only to release her to another mother is no small task. To nurture a child whom you may never see again instead of choosing the grisly options offered by our culture of convenience is a sure sign of love.

And then this child received even more love. Adoptive parents go to extreme lengths to seek out their child. They open their homes and lives to this little one with eager expectation and sheer rejoicing. This is their child.

No parent understands this seeking as

much as God Himself: "You did not choose Me, but I chose you" (John 15:16). We are His children, and He wants the best for us. "I am the LORD; I have called you in righteousness; I will take you by the hand and keep you" (Isaiah 42:6). Our loving Father, our Abba, calls us, loves us, and leads us. Even when we turn away or try to reject our place as children of God, He forgives us and brings us back home.

Consider reading through the prayer "Waiting for an Adoption" in the Topical Prayers section. As you contemplate the love adoptive parents have for their children, think also of the love Your Father has for you and your family.

A LIFE OF JOY

Rejoice in the Lord always; again I will say, rejoice. *Philippians 4:4*

$\mathcal{E}$ ven at a tiny age, my daughter seemed to be full of joy. In fact, I often told others that she was joy personified. This obvious hyperbole nevertheless made me smile as I watched my girl bounce from person to person, a broad smile beaming across her face. Her bold confessions of faith after Sunday School, during church, and in the grocery store are delivered with sincere happiness. In fact, her cheerful demeanor is a gift to our family because it is also contagious. It takes great effort to remain grumpy when happy songs are floating through the room or sunny pictures lie scattered across the just-straightened living room floor.

But I can sure try.

Even in the midst of God's many gifts, I let my face sulk and my shoulders slack in frustration or fatigue. I hate to admit it, but my lack of joy often leads me to turn my sour attitude toward some of my greatest gifts in life—my family, even my little joy. Sadly, my grouchiness is contagious too.

But we Christians, of all people, have reason to be rejoicing with every breath we have. Like the preschool choir who belts out a song

about Jesus with unrestrained mirth, like the student who brings his friend to confirmation class, like the youth who participates in a servant activity—we have every reason to be full of joy. Our sins and sorrows are nailed to the cross, and we live in the joy of Easter morning. In this sinful world, however, we experience sorrow. We grow weary. We even let our sinful nature breed discontent and ill will. Through all these times, however, we can know the sure joy of God's love. We can repent of the times our discontent is our own fault, and we can receive forgiveness for those times. Even when the world is making us weary, we can witness to the joy and hope that God gives. Rejoice! By God's grace, let us overflow with joy in our lives so that others seek for its Source.

Even if it isn't Tuesday, consider using the "Tuesday" prayer in the General Prayers section of this book because of its theme. You may also consider using a message board or posting a large piece of paper on your refrigerator this week. Ask your family members what things give them joy. Write some yourself as well. Throughout the week, watch the list grow; end the week with a prayer of joy and thanksgiving. When you find yourself feeling unhappy, turn to your Lord in prayer. Go back to the list of joy and remember His many gifts to you.

JOY IN THE WALK

I have no greater joy than to hear that my children are walking in the truth.   *3 John 1:4*

*T*here's a reason why the pews are packed when the Sunday School participates in a Christmas service. It's not hard to find the smiles when a child belts out the Lord's Prayer during worship. When youth share their recent servant experience with their congregation, it is an uplifting time.

It is a joy to see God's children of any age when they walk in the truth. John is talking to believers of all ages in the passage above, but parents and grandparents and adults throughout the church can relate to the joy John describes here. When a new generation expresses the love they share because of Jesus' love for them, it is a beautiful moment for those who witness.

"Train up a child in the way he should go; even when he is old he will not depart from it" (Proverbs 22:6). We all know that sin seeks to distract believers of all ages from the salvation they have through Jesus Christ. It is, therefore, all the more powerful for generations to witness to one another the Gospel message of our Savior. When the old share with the young, they are giving the most valuable heirloom they possess. When the young share with the old, they edify their fellow believers and encourage them with ancient words made new.

Let us express that joy to the young when we witness their testimony of faith. Let us encourage them to proclaim God's Word even more. Let us pray for them as they face the challenges of a sinful world. And let us, by the power of the Holy Spirit, demonstrate that same love to those of all ages.

Consider singing "Let Us Ever Walk with Jesus" in the Hymns section of this book. Do you know a particularly joyful child? Thank the Lord for his or her happy witness.

COPYCAT

> For I have given you an example,
> that you also should do just as I
> have done to you. *John 13:15*

A copycat is not always a good thing; we've heard our children use the term as an accusation in the midst of frustration and annoyance. But there are times when copycats give us joy. We stop short, realizing that our kids are imitating us—in a good way.

This is especially true when they follow our example of faith. We smile when we see our daughter leading her friends in a prayer before they eat pizza. We thank God when our son leaves a party that has become questionable in nature. We celebrate when the words we once used to tell of God's love tumble from the lips of our maturing kids.

This is not the first generation of copycats, of course. Throughout history, God has used His people to tell one another of His love and to pass along His Word to the world. "Join in imitating me," Paul tells the Philippians, "and keep your eyes on those who walk according to the example you have in us" (3:17). In the passage at the beginning of this devotion, Jesus was encouraging His disciples to follow His example of service. Paul tells new believers to follow him and other Christians in the ways of their Lord. We are reading devotions—probably because someone encouraged this behavior in us. And our children see our example too. It is a joy for believers to see other children of God reach out and become shining examples in the dark world.

Just like any imitation, we cannot perfectly follow our perfect God. But with the help of the Holy Spirit, we can share that forgiveness of Christ with one another and lead others to follow Christ. One day, all generations will rejoice together as we follow and worship the Lord in heaven.

Think about reading Psalm 1 in the Psalms section of this book. In that same section, read Psalm 24:11. Pray that the Lord guide you in guiding your children so that they may be guides to others as well.

CROWN OF THE AGED

Grandchildren are the crown of
the aged, and the glory of children
is their fathers.   *Proverbs 17:6*

*H*ey, Gramps, can you hurry up a little?" It's strange that our culture does not always honor grandparents and aging adults. One reason might be that grandparents themselves do not honor their own vocation: "Don't you dare call me Grandma! I'm not that old."

But the Bible is clear that aging can be a blessing. "Wisdom is with the aged, and understanding in length of days" (Job 12:12). To be sure, wisdom is not a surefire guaranteed byproduct of the aging process, but many of us learn as we live our lives, growing in our faith. As a result, we accumulate a lifetime of wise attributes: patience, humility, and trust, to name a few. This learning is not an entitlement or something to gloat over, but rather an opportunity to model Christian living and service to others.

"Grandchildren are the crown of the aged." How true that can be! The experience of sharing time and love with those much younger can impact both child and adult. And many adults without children or grandchildren of their own can be true blessings to young families. Consider the woman who sits near a young family in church to lend a helping hand instead of a reproving scowl. Consider the neighbor who teaches gardening to the children on the other side of the fence. Even in (and maybe especially in) the later years of life, we can share our joy in the Lord with others. Often, that joy is returned and multiplied to us.

Consider praying the prayer "For Home and Family" in the Topical Prayers section of this book. Keep particular families in mind as you pray. Are there families nearby you can help in some way? Find ways to offer your support. Are there older adults in your life? Consider ways to share your family joys with them.

Sorrow in Parenting

Sorrow in My Heart

How long must I take counsel in
my soul and have sorrow in my
heart all the day? How long shall
my enemy be exalted over me?
Consider and answer me, O Lord
my God; light up my eyes.

Psalm 13:2–3

My heart ached as I sat in a circle of women, each with tears in their eyes. One mother grieved over the loss of her son, who had died as a toddler decades before in a tragic accident. Two other women shared the agony of never meeting their children face-to-face and carrying the grief of a lost child few others knew even existed. As time drew on that evening, my phone began to vibrate in fits. Despite dismal cell phone reception, I learned through broken texts and voicemails that my dear friend had just lost her own child only a few weeks into pregnancy and was going through great physical and emotional pain. Brokenhearted, I mourned with my sisters who had lost their babies days, years, and decades ago. I knew that these women and their husbands would continue to mourn throughout their earthly lives.

Whether we know it or not, most of us are touched by miscarriage, tragedy, and infertility. Whether we acknowledge it or not, we have hurting friends and family members who grieve over the children they lost and the children they never had.

For this reason, I never ask others about their plans for children. I cringe when well-meaning inquirers hint to a couple that the time for a family has come. Perhaps I should be more open in talking about such things, but I am wary of the emotional landmines I might drag others into with such conversation. How do you tell a lunchtime group that your precious child died a few years ago, with no wit-

nesses but the hospital staff and a few family members? How do you explain to a new acquaintance that you're not *really* an only child without sharing a story full of sadness?

On the other hand, this silence can lead those who are hurting to believe that they are alone. If this applies to you, recall Hannah, whose prayers for a son were full of bitter tears. Think of Bathsheba, who watched her son die after a week of suffering. Don't forget Anna, who never held her own child in her arms. Certainly don't overlook your heavenly Father, who watched His Son agonize over the pain and shame of a horrifying death in front of His murderers.

You are not alone.

In this world of sin, death claims every single one of us and every single one of our loved ones. We may lose our children in secret, in battle, or through tragedy, but too many of us will see the death of our loved ones before we see our own.

You are not alone.

God sees the sorrow of your heart, and He knows intimately how you feel. He saw His Son die, and He grieves for the deaths of all His children. But He will light up your eyes. Death will meet its own demise someday, and our tears will disappear for eternity when we see the life God has prepared for us. In heaven, we will be reunited with all of God's children and with Jesus, the Son who took the place for us all.

As you continue your time of devotion today, consider praying "By the Bereaved" in the

Topical Prayers section. You may also want to read Isaiah 63:7–9 in the Scripture Texts section.

OUR HEALER

> Then shall your light break forth
> like the dawn, and your healing
> shall spring up speedily; your
> righteousness shall go before you;
> the glory of the LORD shall be your
> rear guard. Then you shall call, and
> the LORD will answer; you shall cry,
> and He will say, "Here I am."
>
> *Isaiah 58:8–9*

It's one thing to be sick or in pain. It's a different thing altogether to see your child suffer. Maybe it's his first time to experience a cold or the flu, and he doesn't understand why you can't make it better. Maybe the first scrape brings tears to your eyes more than to hers. Maybe your middle school son is on the soccer sidelines; his usual gait halted by a cast. Maybe your teen is missing out on her last summer before college because of an infection that won't go away. Or maybe your child has been ill since before he was born and doesn't even know how it feels to be healthy.

Such suffering is painful for all around, and it can be difficult to comfort those who need it. How do you talk about cancer to your preschooler? How do you explain multiple sclerosis to an older brother? The pain then creeps into the hearts of the parents until there seems to be no cure.

You know that Jesus suffered on the cross. Does it seem a little too real now that you see pain in your own family? You know that God the Father watched His Son die. Do you fear that you will have a similar heartache? It may seem too easy to say, but God really *does* know how you feel. And He feels pain knowing what you're going through too. And He brings healing. He can restore the sick, the paralyzed, the dying. He can bring comfort to the fearful, the hurting, the mourning. And whether He restores immediately or years from now or when He raises all of us on the Last Day, we know that He takes joy in bringing eternal life to all His people. One day, none of us will feel pain anymore, and we will rejoice together with bodies made perfect.

There are several prayers that may help you today. In the Topical Prayers section, consider "Care for an Ailing Child," "For the Sick," and "For Patience While Recovering." After praying one or more of these, write down a prayer of your own. Revisit this prayer later, and see how God has worked in your life. Do you want to rewrite it now?

WHAT A FRIEND

In the world you will have tribulation. But take heart; I have overcome the world. *John 16:33*

"Why don't those boys and girls like me?" The question varies, but it's never easy. Your precious child, whom you love dearly, is cast aside by his or her peers. They ignore her. They tease him. They don't see the immense value in your child, and the heartbreak she feels causes your own.

Sometimes a hug or a diversion will help. Other times, the problem lasts for weeks until every day seems like a challenge to remind your son that he is special.

Jesus knows what it is to be ignored, ridiculed, betrayed, and denied. The taunts from the very people He helped made Him no less of a person, no less our God. But the persecution still hurts, no matter how unfounded it is.

Jesus assured His followers that their lives would be difficult. Believing in God will not rescue us from trouble. In fact, it often provokes it: "Blessed are you when others revile you and persecute you and utter all kinds of evil against you falsely on My account" (Matthew 5:11). Our Savior is honest: we will have trouble, especially because we are Christians. But our Creator sees us as His dearly loved children, and our Redeemer paid the ultimate price on our behalf. Our Helper, the Holy Spirit, lifts us up and enables us to continue each day—no matter the obstacles we face.

Jesus is our faithful friend. Remind your children—and yourself—that Jesus is with us even when we feel all alone. During family devotion time, consider singing "What a Friend We Have in Jesus" from the Hymns section of this book. If you need to read a similar message tomorrow, look for "Rejected" in the Peace in Parenting portion of this Meditations section.

TURNING AWAY

> Be not wise in your own eyes; fear the LORD, and turn away from evil.
>
> *Proverbs 3:7*

It's painful to see your child sick. It's devastating to watch your child die. But even in these cases, parents are often comforted with the sure hope of the resurrection and life eternal. When our Lord returns, all believers will dwell with Him and with one another. Forever.

The diseased bodies and decayed limbs will be restored; we will sing and dance and embrace one another in perfect joy. How beautiful that picture is!

Unless your child is turning away from the Lord. Suddenly, that certainty is diminished. To know that your child is ignoring his or her true Father—the one who loves him or her most—can provide the kind of sorrow that finds little, if any, relief.

Two fathers have similar stories. Eli, the priest, had two sons. Even though these sons grew up in and served at the Lord's house, they deliberately turned away from God. Eli's discipline was too little and too late, and the Lord rejected the sons as well as Eli (1 Samuel 2:31). Samuel, who had been under Eli's care, also became a father. His sons also turned away (1 Samuel 8:3). But God did not pass the same judgment on Samuel (v. 7). Children do disobey. And though God requires that parents lead their children in the ways of the Lord, obedience is not guaranteed, even by children of godly parents.

It's true that we should hold fast to the words of Proverbs 22:6: "Train up a child in the way he should go; even when he is old he will not depart from it." But sin is pervasive even in the most godly families. Parents who have nurtured their children in God's Word can find comfort in the Lord, as Samuel did. They can pray for their children. They can be living examples of God's patient, forgiving love. They can find strength in the Lord as they witness anew to their sons and daughters. Even if it takes almost a lifetime, those continued parental prayers can ultimately be used by God to turn children *back* to forgiveness and eternal life.

If you're experiencing a similar situation, consider the prayer "Care for a Difficult Child" in the Topical Prayers section. Pray also for all Christian families, that the adults make God's Word and His will the first priority in raising their children.

NEVER ALONE

And behold, I am with you always,

to the end of the age.

First comes love, then comes marriage, then comes the baby in the baby carriage. Then comes divorce. Or there's death—wait. This childhood rhyme has gone terribly wrong. As we grow up, most of us hear about family basics, either from childhood anecdotes such as this one, from parents, or perhaps from God Himself: "Therefore a man shall leave his father and his mother and hold fast to his wife, and they shall become one flesh" (Genesis 2:24). Although our cultural assertions are to the contrary, God's intentions for a family are understood by believers. A man and woman vow to be faithful in marriage, which often leads them to become parents—a team as they raise their children.

But sin interferes with all good things here on earth, and God's gift of family seems especially under attack. A husband is unfaithful. A wife deserts her family. A tragic death claims a mom or dad. Suddenly, the "happy family" picture is distorted into a scene of pain and longing.

Not only do single parents suffer the emotional loss of losing a trusted partner, but they also are left to comfort their reeling children. Further, they must continue to do the normal tasks of raising a family—and do so alone. Grief multiplies until the burden begins to feel too heavy to handle.

"Cast your burden on the LORD, and He will sustain you" (Psalm 55:22). Our God sees your pain, and He promises to bear it for you. In fact, He already has. Jesus took the sins that break families apart; He took all the mistakes we've ever made. And He carried them. He bore them on His shoulders and nailed them to the cross. He died for all of us so that our pasts—yet to come thousands of years later— would already be cast on Him. Sharing our burdens and healing our pains, Jesus promises to be with us to the very end.

Consider reading the prayers "During Tragedy" or "By the Bereaved," found in the

Topical Prayers section. If these words apply to you, take comfort in the promise of the Lord's love for you. If you know of someone who is grappling with loss, think of reaching out and praying these prayers with that person. Ask how you can help, witnessing to Christ's love for His people.

I HAVE SINNED

I have sinned against the LORD.

2 Samuel 12:13

When our children are little, we are heroes. We are invincible. We are infallible. In their eyes, that is. In reality, we are just as sinful as anyone else, including the stubborn toddler or apathetic teenager. Sometimes, the faith our children have in us prompts us to go along with the illusion. We hide our sins; we deny our faults.

It doesn't take long, however, for our children to see the truth. And if we continue to fail to admit our failures, they begin to distrust us.

Instead of pointing our children to have faith in their perfect Savior, we put up a pathetic show of prideful theatrics that inevitably fall flat.

And as if this wasn't bad enough, our sin can do even worse. We often fail to see it, but our sin almost never limits its damage to us. Many of the sorrows we've read about in this book happen outside of our control. Often, however, the grief our family endures is directly due to our own actions.

Maybe our failure to focus on family leads our children to feel alone and without guidance. Maybe our addiction saps away all energy and resources from what could have been a healthy childhood. Maybe our spiritual laziness encourages our children to forget the importance of their heavenly Father. Maybe our unfaithfulness shakes our family foundation to its core. Maybe our selfishness allows us to abandon the marriage that supported our child's well-being. Maybe our lack of hope has prompted us to even kill the unborn child we were meant to protect.

No. Sin is not content to cause suffering for the sinner only. It injures everyone around, leaving them feeling grief, pain, and betrayal. And it's your fault. It's my fault. We, the parents, are the cause for our children's sorrow—multiplying our own grief.

David was one of the Old Testament stars, if you will. He walked with God. He was the Lord's anointed. He is a type, a foreshadowing, for Jesus Himself, the Son of David. *And yet he, too, sinned.* In fact, David broke every commandment, and he tried to hide it all (e.g., 2 Samuel 11). When finally faced with the truth, David could only admit his sin. He was responsible for death and pain and family strife—just to name a few consequences. *And yet he, too, was forgiven.* In an honest psalm of confession, David admits, "I know my transgressions." He begs, "Create in me a clean heart, O God." And he rejoices, "My mouth will declare Your praise" (Psalm 51:3, 10, 15). When we sin, we can confess to our Father and to our family. We can find comfort and cleansing in the forgiveness of our Savior. We can find reconciliation by the Spirit of our God.

Is your sin hurting you and your family? You may want to pray "For Deliverance from Sin" or "For Help in Time of Temptation," found in the Topical Prayers section. David was confronted with his sin by Nathan. If you, like Nathan, need to speak with someone who is bound secure in his or her sin, pray to God for wisdom in approaching that person.

FEAR IN PARENTING

WHEN YOU PASS THROUGH THE WATERS

Fear not, for I have redeemed you;
I have called you by name, you
are Mine. When you pass through
the waters, I will be with you; and
through the rivers, they shall not
overwhelm you; when you walk
through fire you shall not be
burned, and the flame shall not
consume you. For I am the LORD
your God, the Holy One of Israel,
your Savior.   *Isaiah 43:1–3*

At some point, it happens. Instead of reading the pregnancy self-help book, you read the newest tragedy emblazoned in the newspaper headline. Or you're holding your child in the pediatrician's waiting room when you overhear two people talking about a crime that oc-

© iStockphoto.com

curred a few blocks from your neighborhood. Or maybe you take a break while your little one naps and find only crass commercials and hopeless shows on the TV screen.

In the midst of your parenting joy, the ugliness of this sinful world interrupts the happiness you have and allows fear to creep in. How can you raise a child in this terrible place? Is there anything you can do to prevent all harm to your precious son or daughter? What if something bad happens?

God tells His children that "what if" is not the question. He talks about "when you pass through the waters" and "when you walk through fire." Because of this sinful world, all of God's people will face hardships and trial. As much as we try to tune out the troubles of our world, we cannot deny that bad things are inevitable.

And the harder truth is that, as sinful children of God, we deserve so much more than the difficulties we may face. We deserve God's eternal anger just as much as the Israelites did when Isaiah shared the message above thousands of years ago.

But our Father has mercy. Yes, we will face water and fire and flame, but we will not be overwhelmed or burned or consumed. "Fear not," our Lord tells us (v. 1). "I am . . . your Savior" (v. 3).

Try as we might, we cannot shield our children from every bad thing that may come their way. They will get bruises and hurt feelings. They will see pain and death. But our Lord is with them—and us—as He was with the Israelites. He has redeemed us through Jesus, and we are His.

Think of some of the fears you are facing right now. If you can, write them down. Now, read Isaiah 63:7–9 in the Scripture Texts section; consider the ways God "lifted up" and "carried" His people long ago (v. 9). Can He do similar things for you? Look back at what you wrote down, and pray to God for help and strength. If you have time, read or sing "O God, Forsake Me Not," which you can find in the Hymns section of this book.

ANXIOUSLY AWAITING

The Lord is at hand; do not be anxious about anything, but in everything by prayer and supplication with thanksgiving let your requests be made known to God. And the peace of God, which surpasses all understanding, will guard your hearts and your minds in Christ Jesus.   *Philippians 4:5–7*

A quick Internet search about parenting

fears pulls up a plethora of possibilities to worry over. One mom wrote an entertaining article that included forty-nine of the parenting fears she experienced in one week. Many of them sound eerily familiar.

Why is it that parenting suddenly brings out all kinds of irrational fears and worries that we had never considered before? Perhaps the fact that another life is in our hands causes us to wring them persistently, awaiting any disaster that may come. (I wonder how God would look if He wrung His hands for every life that was in His hands.)

That Internet search certainly provided plenty to perplex any parent. But the solutions to such fears were sadly lacking. Most of them pointed back to the parents and their power to relax. But most of us know that we are poor consolation when we're anxious. That's why we're searching for calming blogs and articles in the first place! Paul points to someone else.

"Do not be anxious about anything," says the man who had faced prison and persecution. "The Lord is at hand." Back to that earlier thought about God's hands. We are in His hands, and He isn't worried. He knows that He is in control, and He invites us to bring all our concerns to Him. He will bring us comfort.

Instead of passively waiting for our fears to be a reality or looking inward for some hidden strength, we can look to the Lord and see that He is present and ready to provide protection. Yes, our children are in our hands. But we are all in the hands of our Father.

If you have time, turn to the Hymns section of this book and read the fourth stanza to "Go, My Children, with My Blessing." You may want to learn it by heart and sing it with your family during your bedtime routine. God has been saying similar words of comfort since Moses' time, and He says them to you today.

MURKY MORNINGS

O LORD, God of my salvation; I cry out day and night before You.

Psalm 88:1

It's not easy to see your child sick or in pain. You want to fix the problem immediately, but it can take time—time for a diagnosis, time for the medicine to kick in, time for healing. Psychological and emotional troubles can be especially hard because the symptoms are not always easy for others to recognize. The child and parents are often left feeling alone—experiencing a spectrum of emotions throughout any given day.

One parent paints such a picture: "Well, this morning, there was joy when singing to my daughter to wake her, sorrow when I could see that she was suffering from anxiety and tiredness, fear thinking about her future, stress while my husband and I talked about a plan of action, and peace when I gave it all to Jesus." And repeat. The cycle of emotions can leave the entire family exhausted, running out of places to turn.

The parent continues, "Sometimes when the pain is so strong and cutting, it's hard to see the One who cares for you; it's impossible to know that you are not alone. This is where the habits we develop as Christians kick in. We know we're supposed to read Scripture and pray, so we do, even if we can't see the words on the page through all the tears. And sometimes we have to live those habits for quite a while before we feel His presence again. Not because He hasn't been there but because we have sunk so deep into our misery that we can't see Him."

Those who advise to follow your heart must not have ever been betrayed by its fickle wanderings. Those who look to their logic for guidance must not have ever experienced those moments when the mind fails. We can't even trust ourselves when psychological struggles shake our lives, leaving our hearts aching with grief.

No matter what our hearts and minds say, though, God's Word never lies. Even when we can't hear His voice, we know our Lord promises to be true. Jesus, who experienced the most horrible agony for us, is always by our side—and He will not let go. As morning after morning we wait for healing, we trust in our God, who never fails.

Consider the words "I Am Trusting Thee, Lord Jesus" in the Hymns section of this book. You may also want to pray "Care for an Ailing Child" or "Care for a Difficult Child" in the Topical Prayers section. If you know a family who is suffering through psychological challenges, ask for ways to help them. Keep them in your prayers.

Practically an Adult

> May our sons in their youth be like
> plants full grown, our daughters
> like corner pillars cut for the struc-
> ture of a palace. *Psalm 144:12*

It's bound to happen. "Mama" turns to "Mommy" and then "Mom." "Dada" turns to "Daddy" and then "Dad." Then "Mom" and "Dad" get two syllables each: "Mo-om, I'm not a child anymore." "Da-ad, I'm practically an adult!"

There are blessings to this development. We don't want a lifetime of diapers; we're happy

© iStockphoto.com

that our kids can read. Independence and responsibility are great outcomes, right?

But as our family members grow, there can be conflict during those stages. We focus on *practically* while they focus on *adult*. We focus on *responsibility* while they focus on *independence*. It seems that as our children get closer and closer to adulthood, we get less and less prepared for it.

Sure, deep down, we want our children to drive. to work. to date. to grow up. But there are so many dangers in this sinful world, and our fear of a scraped knee or a bad habit is exchanged for new fears of car accidents and drug abuse. It's almost enough to cause us to lock the doors and hide the car keys! For many of us, we replace the time we used to spend *playing* with our kids with *worrying* about them.

But just as we grew up, so our kids need to grow up too. And the Lord who keeps us safe promises to protect our children as well. Sin is inevitable, but God's love is unconditional. "For I, the LORD your God, hold your right hand; it is I who say to you, 'Fear not, I am the one who helps you'" (Isaiah 41:13). Our Father promises this to us, and He promises this to our children. We can turn our times of fear into times of prayer, our times of worry into times of trust, for our God keeps His promises.

Write down the fears you have about your teenager, and pray to God about them. When you pray for your child, let him or her know you are doing so; demonstrate your trust in the Lord regarding your children. Consider praying "Care for Teenage Children" in the Topical Prayers section of this book.

FAMILY FEUDS

Refrain from anger, and forsake
wrath! Fret not yourself; it tends
only to evil.   *Psalm 37:8*

*F*or many of us, family is a safe place. It is where we find love, comfort, and understanding. Even if the rest of the world is against us, we seek solace in our family.

But sin loves to infect families. Sin *targets* families because God gave this special gift to us; the devil wants nothing more than to destroy God's sweetest blessings. Some of us have experienced abuse and struggle and have repeated the same pattern with others. Some of us avoid certain relatives for the sake of our children. Some of us watch our own children rise up against each other as they grow older. Such suffering in a family can cut so deep that it undermines our own relationship with God.

God. Now, He's one who knows about family struggles. He witnessed it with Cain and Abel. Leah and Rebekah. Saul and Jonathan.

Even more, He sees it in us, His disobedient and quarreling children. We fight with Him; we fight with our brothers and sisters in Christ. We're an unhappy, feuding family.

And because of the separation we caused, God separated Himself from—even forsook— His own Son. He completely refused to help His Son, Jesus, as He hung on the cross. Yes, our Father knows the pain in families. And He also knows reconciliation. When Jesus paid our price and rose again, He welcomed us back to the family. Our Father waits with open arms as we reunite with Him and the rest of our huge, heavenly family.

On earth, we may never see the renewal that we so desperately want in our families. But because of the Son, we are able to show love even in the most hateful situations. We can witness to the loving Father so that our brothers and sisters can receive restoration as well.

Find "Amazing Grace" in the Hymns section of this book, and reflect on the familiar words slowly. Read them with your family.

Thank God for His grace and love for sinners. You may want to read the "Friday" prayer in the General Prayers section of this book as well. As you close, think about those who are unloving toward you. Pray for them.

NOT FORGOTTEN

Remember these things, O Jacob,
and Israel, for you are My servant;
I formed you; you are My servant;
O Israel, you will not be forgotten
by Me. I have blotted out your
transgressions like a cloud and
your sins like mist; return to Me,
for I have redeemed you.

Isaiah 44:21–22

After the waiting, the diapers, the smiles, the teething, the kisses, the tantrums, the paintings, the scraped knees, the trophies, the bullies, the best friends, the first breakup, the first car—after a childhood full of experiences, it ends. Sure, you are still a parent. That remains throughout your earthly life. But suddenly, your children move on. "Therefore a man shall leave his father and his mother and hold fast to his wife, and they shall become one flesh" (Genesis 2:24). This kind of separation seemed natural to you when you were doing the leaving. But now, you're the one left behind.

And then there are the phone calls and the visits and the texts and the grandkids and the job promotions—but the contact is not as often as you'd like. You're now watching it from the sidelines, helping where you can and resisting the urge to do too much.

You begin to wonder: Am I forgotten? What will happen to me? Whom can I take care of? Who will take care of me?

As we age, our vocations change. When our roles as parent and employee and volunteer begin to fade, we wonder what's next in life. We wonder if we're needed. If we're wanted.

But as long as we have breath, there is a reason why we're here. Our Lord yearns for us to return to Him, so our time on earth is for a purpose. We can help. We can model patience. We can smile. We can pray for others. We can receive care from those who need to serve. And through it all, we are still very loved sons and daughters. "Beloved, we are God's children" (1 John 3:2).

Consider praying "Care for Adult Children" from the Topical Prayers section of this book. Pray for your children and family, wherever they are. Pray that you remember your Father's eternal love for you.

STRESS IN PARENTING

BE STILL

> Be still before the Lord and wait
> patiently for Him. . . . Fret not your-
> self; it tends only to evil.
>
> *Psalm 37:7–8*

*W*ill you just hold still?" It's a question we find ourselves asking our children all too frequently, isn't it? When changing a diaper, pulling on an outfit, fixing hair, wiping a face, applying a bandage, we ask our children to *be still* so that we can help them. "You're just making it worse. Be patient!"

If only we could take our own advice. Sometimes, I imagine our children saying the same to us. In fact, they often do. "Mommy, can you play with me?" "Daddy, I need your help." "Grandma, look at this!" Even the fussy baby who won't let you get up to wipe down the counter seems to say, "Slow down! Just hold me for a while."

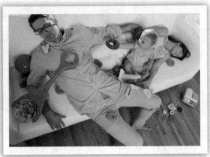

Why are we so hesitant to be still? Why do we fret? If we wrote down the reasons and situations, I think we would find many excuses.

"I'd like to stop and play, but I have too many tasks on my to-do list today. Someone won't think I'm productive enough if I stop what I'm doing."

"My peers seem so much further in life right now. It doesn't seem fair that they're doing so well and I'm just lagging behind."

"I'm in charge of another life now. If I let go of the control I have (or think I have) for just one minute, who knows what will happen?"

"No one is listening to what I need or what I

have to say. I've just gotta do everything myself around here."

Do any of these sound familiar? Do you have others? Take a moment and look at the pronouns in these phrases that so often come to mind. Who is the focus? I. Me. My. When we neglect to be still, we are forgetting the other people in our lives. Even more, we're forgetting the One who tells us to be still. We hear "be still" again in Psalm 46:10: "Be still, and know that I am God."

As hard as it may be, add a new point or two to that to-do list. Be still, and spend time with your Lord. Be still, and remember that He is in control. Be still, and enjoy the gifts He has given you—including your family. You might be surprised at how that to-do list will get re-prioritized when "be still" is part of it.

Think about the reasons that prevent you from being still. What is really at the root of these reasons? Be still, and pray to God for help. You might get pretty good at "being still," but you'll fall short too. God forgives you and gives you a rest that comes only from your Savior. Consider reading the prayer for "Vocation" in the Topical Prayers section of this book.

DOING THE RIGHT THING

> This Book of the Law shall not
> depart from your mouth, but you
> shall meditate on it day and night,
> so that you may be careful to do
> according to all that is written in
> it. For then you will make your
> way prosperous, and then you will
> have good success.   *Joshua 1:8*

Don't eat chocolate while you're pregnant. Eat anything you want. Lay your baby on his belly. No, on his back. Make sure your toddler gets plenty of sensory exposure. Don't overwhelm her with too many sensory experiences. Get your preschooler involved in sports activities. Don't register him for a team until grade school. Kids don't get outside enough these days. Don't you dare let your child out of your sight under any circumstance. Let your teenager date early on so you can supervise. Dating is dangerous and should be avoided until adulthood.

Parents get plenty of advice. Baby books, magazines, mommy blogs, social-networking posts, grandparent laments, and plenty of other sources provide so much information about the "right" way to parent, there only seems to be a long, long, long list of the "wrong" things you can do. Which book should you follow? Which should you disregard?

Joshua has a suggestion: "The Book of the Law shall not depart from your mouth." Did you just drop this book in despair over more impossible advice? Thanks for picking it back up again. Let's try to explore what this difficult passage might mean.

First of all, the scary-sounding "Book of the Law" means the Bible that Joshua and the Israelites had at the time—the Torah, the Pentateuch, the first five books of the Bible. So Joshua is impressing upon the people the importance of the Bible—something they had known in their hearts but never held in their hands or seen with their eyes until just recently as Moses wrote it down.

Okay, yes, you may be thinking. *The Bible is important. Check. It's more important than magazines or blogs or parenting books. Sure. But it cannot depart from my mouth? I need to meditate on it day and night? I have to do* all *that's written in it? And then I'll have success?*

Did you throw this book down again?

I wonder if the people of Israel were feeling the same thing. They knew that their parents had failed miserably in following the Lord. How can they possibly be so faithful? It's a good thing that Joshua followed his words quickly with a message of comfort: "Do not be frightened, and do not be dismayed, for the LORD your God is with you wherever you go" (v. 9).

When the online news feeds begin to clutter with differing parenting opinions, we can turn to God's Word. When the parenting books overwhelm us, we can find comfort in His love. And when we are convicted that we don't take our Father's messages to heart, we can know that He forgives us and stays with us wherever we go. He'll guide our steps as we guide the steps of our children.

If you have a moment, turn to "Loving Father, Guide Your Children" in the Hymns section and meditate on the words. It's a newer hymn; you can use the suggested tune, if you'd like to sing it. If any lines in particular resonate with you today, spend some time in prayer about what comes to mind.

THE DAILY PLANNER

For my days pass away like smoke. . . . I forget to eat my bread.

Psalm 102:3–4

*W*here is your to-do list? Are you hiding from it at the moment? Is it distracting you from this devotion right now? Maybe it's pages long: laundry, baseball, piano, 4-H, homework, cooking, cleaning, work, and so on and on and on. Maybe you don't even write it down because you can't spare a moment to find a pen.

As our kids begin to grow, they take on more roles and responsibilities. Which means you do as well. Sometimes, the tasks we have taken for ourselves and for our family get so overwhelming that we want to cry, or days pass by and we forget to eat. Or sleep. Or pray.

The schedule of a parent never seems to be easy; it just changes as our children age. We lose track of our days, weeks, months, years. "But You, O LORD, are enthroned forever; You are remembered throughout all generations" (v. 12). When our daily planner becomes a wreck, we can remember our eternal God, who has led His people throughout the ages. When our days on earth end, we know that our lives continue forever—*countless* days—with our Lord.

In the meantime, let us make the most of our days—especially when we schedule time to rest and meditate on God's Word alone as well as with our children. We can find rest in the assurance that all God's people will spend their days together with Him. "The children of Your servants shall dwell secure; their offspring shall be established before You" (v. 28).

Gather your family together to look at the week ahead. When can you schedule time to share in God's Word? Consider singing "By Your Life, O Lord, We Live," found in the Hymns section of this book.

God's Planning

> For I know the plans I have for you,
> declares the LORD, plans for welfare
> and not for evil, to give you a
> future and a hope.   *Jeremiah 29:11*

Educators and parents both know that one of the easiest times for disruption is during a transition time. If transitions from one activity to another go smoothly, children are more likely to go along without complaint or misbehavior.

But what a stress those transitions can

be! Moving from one room to another is one thing. Moving from one day to another is pretty easy. But then you get the whoppers: changing schools, changing friends, changing cities, changing lives.

It would be tempting to try to avoid transitions altogether! But any teacher knows that a day without variety is just as troublesome. And families are meant to change too. Families grow. Kids age. Things change.

The toughest transitions are probably those we don't plan for. Surprises enter our lives, giving us mental whiplash and causing us to wonder what the next turn will bring. "We didn't prepare for this!" we tell God. "How will we get through this?" we wonder. "Where are You taking us, Lord?" we ask.

When life seems out of control, we panic over what transitions we're facing. But during those times, we are reminded that we're *never* really in control—and that's a real comfort. Our Father, who is always in control of our lives, never changes. He promises to bring you through all your stages in life "to give you a future and a hope." Ultimately, the final transition will be when all God's children rise again and gather for an eternal and blessed family reunion.

Are you going through a time of transition? Gather your family together and discuss your fears. Pray about them together. Consider reading Psalm 37:23–26 in the Psalms section of this book. Reflect on biblical families who went through transitions, and thank God for His unchanging love. You may want to finish by singing "Let Us Ever Walk with Jesus," found in the Hymns section of this book.

REBEL CHILD

> He . . . appointed a law in Israel,
> which He commanded our fathers
> to teach to their children, that
> the next generation might know
> them, the children yet unborn,
> and arise and tell them to their
> children, so that they should set
> their hope in God . . . and that they

should not be like their fathers, a
stubborn and rebellious generation, a generation whose heart
was not steadfast, whose spirit
was not faithful to God.

Psalm 78:5–8

*R*ebellion. That word carries so many con-
notations—of war, of independence, of pain, of
freedom. When parents think of their children
rebelling, they become filled with fear. When
parents think of their own rebellion, however,
they often chuckle with nostalgia or swell with
pride. To some, it's a mere rite of passage—
foreshadowed in the terrible twos and culmi-
nating as teens become adults. But too many of
us know that rebellion can go terribly wrong.
Rebellion is as old as sin itself, and it is not
something to be taken lightly. Adam and Eve
discovered the horrible repercussions of rebellion. So did Korah. So did Jonah. So do we.

Whether we are the instigators or recipi-
ents of rebellion, we are hurt by the fallout that
comes when rebels turn from God and His will.

As parents, we are filled with stress and fear when we realize what may happen to our kids when they refuse to obey. When we are tempted to lose patience with our children, however, we can remember what God has done for His rebellious people for generations: "I will heal them and reveal to them abundance of prosperity and security. . . . I will cleanse them from all the guilt of their sin against Me, and I will forgive all the guilt of their sin and rebellion against Me" (Jeremiah 33:6, 8).

Despite our repeated, unrelenting rebellion, God still forgives us when we turn back and confess our sins to Him. Empowered through His Spirit, we can then forgive our rebels when they turn from their ways.

Consider reading Psalm 1 with your family. You can find it in the Psalms section of this book. Can you think of modern examples of the various situations? The Law may weigh down the discussion, but finish with a focus on Jesus, who never once rebelled, but obeyed God's will in order to earn our redemption.

WARNING:
UNCONVENTIONAL FAMILY

> Jesus would die for the nation,
> and not for the nation only,
> but also to gather into one the
> children of God who are scattered
> abroad. *John 11:51–52*

With soaring divorce rates, foster families, international adoptions, unmarried parents, and families with transient parents, it seems as if *conventional* and *typical* are words that cannot possibly be paired with the word *family* anymore. Children have multiple moms or dads. They have no parents at all. They have half-siblings that they barely know. Thanks to the effects that sin has on our world, the word *family* is perhaps more confusing than ever.

Even so, families that are brought together in unusual ways often feel as if they need to explain their special circumstances (warning: unconventional family unit). Parents worry about how to relate to children who are not exactly their own. Grandparents fear that they won't have the energy to raise a second generation into adulthood.

With all of these concerns, it can be comforting to know that God's family is anything but *conventional*. Jesus' own human heritage is riddled with people who wouldn't seem to fit into God's plan for His Son. When reading Jesus' genealogy in Matthew 1 or Luke 3, we see a list of Gentiles, sinners, outcasts, and so on—all in Jesus' family tree. This should not be a surprise, however; God chooses His family from all nations and all times.

Yes, God did have a plan for families—a plan that would not be ruined by death or hate or unfaithfulness. But He also has a plan for salvation—creating a family line for His Son so that He could redeem us all and bring us back to our heavenly Father forever.

Our family lives may not fit the mold God intended. In fact, *all families* and all people fall short of God's expectations. But we can find restoration and forgiveness and unconditional love from our Lord.

In the Scripture Texts section of this book, read Isaiah 54:1–10. Try to picture the family you will have in heaven by thinking of your brothers and sisters in Christ now. Pray for your own family, and pray also for help in serving people of all nations, that they may be God's children.

PEACE IN PARENTING

PEACEFUL PARENTING

> May the LORD give strength to His
> people! May the LORD bless His
> people with peace! *Psalm 29:11*

*P*eace and quiet. It's funny how those two words seem to go together so often. It doesn't take long, however, for anyone to realize that parenting is anything but quiet. In fact, the joke often goes that when children are quiet too long, there's trouble! What happened to those images of serene babes smiling in their sleep or cuddling peacefully with a stuffed animal?

Too quickly, the quiet coos break into grating screams. The playful babble turns to disobedient protests. Eventually, the words of love turn into words of defiance. Sinful nature can turn the most adorable child into a loud, disruptive wailer.

And that's just the children.

How many outbursts of our own do our kids endure? Do our complaints and laments set the tone for too many mornings? Do our impatient shouts rival the argument we're trying to end? Even if we hide our squabbles from little ears, we moan with our friends or groan to our spouses or hurl our gripes begrudgingly to our Father.

Although our sinfulness too often disrupts the peacefulness God offers, He forgives our ungrateful whining. More than that, He invites us to bring our concerns and needs to Him on a daily basis. He lovingly listens to our cries for help, and He gives us strength to endure and peace to enjoy. We are people of peace because of the peace we receive from our Father.

In the midst of the cacophony of our lives, we can find harmony in the beautiful words of our Lord. He wants us to take time out for quiet devotion so that we can find peace and rest in His forgiveness. His Word offers comfort in an otherwise tumultuous world. Our Prince of

Peace will equip us to share His love and peace with others, especially our children, so that we might someday live together forever in eternal peace.

Do you have troubles that are drowning out any sense of peace you may have? Take it to the Lord in prayer. In fact, meditate on the words of the hymn "What a Friend We Have in Jesus," which includes that very promise that we can always "take it to the Lord in prayer." It is found in the Hymns section of this book. Our Lord promises to listen to your prayer, and He will give you peace.

PICTURE OF PEACE

Peace I leave with you; My peace I give to you. Not as the world gives do I give to you. Let not your hearts be troubled, neither let them be afraid. *John 14:27–28*

A well-known story has been told with several variations; here is one version. Two artists decided to have a contest to see which one could paint a more accurate portrayal of peace. The first artist went to extraordinary detail in showing a calm meadow. The sun was warm on the motionless blades of grass. No leaf on the surrounding trees rustled in the breeze. Not a sign of movement was evident in the scene. All was still and serene.

The second artist used slashing strokes to create a violent waterfall, crashing over jagged rocks. Currents churned below in whirlpools and rapids. But in the center, hanging just above the frothy waves, a newborn bird rested in a nest, which was cradled in a sturdy branch. As the story goes, the waterfall artist clearly won.

We want the meadow, don't we? We want a life void of any conflict or obstacle. Or maybe we imagine the painting with smiling faces of a healthy family. A luxurious estate with matching convertibles and a personal maid. A pile of books near a beachside lounge chair near a smooth emerald ocean. Regardless, we usually picture peace with no troubles and with plenty of happiness at hand.

That's what the world wants, at least. But Jesus tells us in the passage above that He does not give as the world gives. Because—let's be honest—the books will get damp and the children will begin to bicker and the mansion will require a fortune in maintenance bills. While we're distracted by the meadowlike images of peace, the clouds begin to form.

Jesus, instead, knows that we will see pain in this world. He doesn't ignore it; He has lived it. He is present with you as you go through it. "Let not your hearts be troubled"—Jesus knows that danger will come. But He has already conquered it. He will preserve you in this world and will keep you safe in His hand when it fades away on the Last Day. He gives you peace on the days that you play referee between your kids. He gives you peace when you take a child to the emergency room. He gives you peace when even your spouse abandons you. He gives you peace when your own image of peace begins to distort in the sinful reality of life. He gives peace that passes all understanding, even when there seems to be no calm in sight.

Even if it isn't Wednesday, consider praying the "Wednesday" prayer in the General Prayers section of this book. If you have time, also read or sing stanza 2 of "Go, My Children, with My Blessing." Are you in need of peace? Entrust your cares to Your loving Father.

BEYOND THE CRAYON BOX

> Now may the God of peace who brought again from the dead our Lord Jesus, the great shepherd of the sheep, by the blood of the eternal covenant, equip you with everything good that you may do His will. *Hebrews 13:20–21*

*E*very fall, stores are swamped as families flood the aisles, searching for school supplies. Three erasable pens—check. Five plastic folders with horizontal pockets in differing colors—check. One box of washable markers (10 count) and one box of crayons (24 count)—check and check.

But parents have another checklist on their minds as well. Is my child emotionally prepared to leave my side every weekday? Will my son be able to make friends with the other students? Will my daughter be able to pay attention during the lessons? Those checks are a little harder to make with confidence.

The God of peace, however, equips us for the task at hand. The God who gave wisdom to Solomon will guide His kindergartners through a year full of firsts. The Lord who brought down the Philistines will enable His middle school children to overcome the adversities of peer pressure and low self-esteem. The Father who brought back to life the great Shepherd of the sheep will supervise all students and teachers and administrators and staff to work according to His will through their vocations.

© iStockphoto.com / Christopher Futcher

As our children pass through the school doors with any number of emotions, we can have peace knowing that our God gives us what we need and keeps us in His care.

Reflect on the words of "Let Children Hear the Mighty Deeds," found in the Hymns section. You may also want to pray "Care for Grade School Children" from the Topical Prayers section. May the Lord grant you and your children peace during this new day of learning.

Rejected

He was despised and rejected
by men; a man of sorrows, and
acquainted with grief; and as
one from whom men hide their
faces He was despised, and we
esteemed Him not. *Isaiah 53:3*

*N*o bullying allowed!" "Bully-free zone." The signs are up and the programs are in place, but we all know that bullying still exists. Sin claims the school halls and gym floors as kids torment other kids. We see it in our children as they begin to sulk when it's time for practice. They mumble "I don't wanna talk about it" when asked about their day.

It's not fair, and it's not right. But bullying continues to cause pain throughout the ages. Joseph was bullied by his brothers. Mordecai was bullied by Haman. Even Jesus Himself was bullied.

In a strange way, this might bring some comfort. The bullies certainly were not right to attack the Son of God. They are also not right to attack our son or daughter. As much as it hurts, we know that the lies of a bully have no merit or truth. There is no fault in the bullied child for the attacks he or she endures.

But when emotions get in the way, rejection and persecution are all we see. We begin to feel hopeless when we or our children are victims. "In the world you will have tribulation," Jesus assures us. There's no way around that. "But take heart; I have overcome the world" (John 16:33). Believers are especially under attack because of our association with the One who was persecuted for our sake. He was spit upon, ridiculed, and provoked. He was whipped, mocked, and killed. When we look at our Savior's suffering, we realize we are to blame for it. We were bullies to the best friend we have— Jesus. But on that cross, He paid for our bullying. He forgave our abuse. On that cross full of torture, He won for us eternal peace. Jesus was victorious, and He never leaves our side as we face our own struggles.

With your family, pray for all who are bullied. Pray for wisdom when faced with bullies. Finish by singing "God Loves Me Dearly," found in the Hymns section of this book. If you haven't read it already, you may soon want to read "What a Friend" in the Sorrow in Parenting portion of the Meditations section.

SOURCE OF PEACE

> May grace and peace be multiplied to you in the knowledge of God and of Jesus our Lord.
>
> *2 Peter 1:2*

*Y*ou may know the song "I've Got Peace like a River." This old spiritual is a catchy one, but how often do we think of the themes behind it? For instance, if peace is a river, where is its source? Where does that peace come from?

So you probably just perked up with a knowing smile and the quick answer: *Jesus*! But let's rephrase this question. Be honest with yourself as you read this. When you need comfort, where do you go? When you want a calm heart, what do you listen to? When you want a swelling river of peace in your soul, what is the source you seek?

Some turn on the TV or laptop to drown out the noise of family life. Others read self-help books or entertainment magazines to escape financial pressures. Chocolate. Wine. Bubble baths. Gardening. Indie music. Friends. We know that this list is not bad. These are often good, little blessings from God as we enjoy the world He has created. But do they give us *peace*? As lovely as these gifts can be, we too often stop short there. We fill our sadness with only empty or temporary things—creating a larger hole than before. We may even get distracted by the lies on the radio or movie or article and lose sight of our peace source altogether.

As parents, we set an example by pretty much everything we do. When your kids see that you're tired, do they see you bow your head in prayer? When they know you are worried, do they hear you read God's Word? When they know hard times are coming, do they witness you surrounding yourself with people who remind you of God's eternal peace? Instead of shielding our children from the struggles we face, we can sometimes use those difficult times to show where true peace is found. "Therefore, since we have been justified by faith, we have peace with God through our Lord Jesus Christ" (Romans 5:1).

May the source of true peace flood your heart with a peace that passes all understanding. You may want to pray "Proper Use of Leisure" in the Topical Prayers section.

THE EMPTY NEST

Young men and maidens together, old men and children! Let them praise the name of the LORD, for His name alone is exalted; His majesty is above earth and heaven.

Psalm 148:12–13

$\mathcal{F}$athers of newborns dream of diaperless nights. Mothers of preschoolers long for fort-less living rooms. Grade school parents tire of the sports schedules, and parents of teenag-ers hold on through every new milestone. But when the house is suddenly silent of any chil-dren, the longing doesn't stop. It just continues, this time in retrospect. All those challenges of yesterday are gilt in a nostalgic hue, and we now look to the past for our desired stage in life.

To be sure, the empty-nest phase is full of challenges. There is, of course, a loneliness that comes with that finally achieved quiet. In addi-tion, parents struggle to adapt to their new pa-rental vocation. We never stop being parents, but we are eventually called to let our children live and act as adults. We are faced with the challenge of knowing *how much* to help, *how much* to advise, *how much* to let go.

We do know one thing: there is never a *too much* when it comes to prayer. Even if we haven't seen her face or heard his voice or read a text from her for ages, we can still pray for our children. We can talk to our Father about what it means to be a father and mother of adults. As each child leaves the nest at different ages and with varying degrees, we can pray for wisdom on how to best guide our son or daughter.

And with that prayer, we can begin to see blessings to this stage of life too. We may be able to have more meaningful conversations than ever with our maturing kids. We may find new time to fill with service we were unable to do before. We may even be able to support younger families as they begin this journey of parenthood. We can look back—not with discontented longing, but with gratitude as we reflect on how God led us and our families throughout the years. We can join with all voices—young and old—to praise our Lord.

Pray for the peace that the Lord gives as you approach each new phase of life. If your children are grown, consider reading "Care for Adult Children" and "Times of Parting" in the Topical Prayers section. Is there a passage or hymn that gives you peace? Consider sharing it with your child in a personal note. If you still have younger children, think about visiting with a recent empty-nest couple you know. You can help each other as you listen and talk together.

PSALMS

Be filled with the Spirit, addressing one another in psalms and hymns and spiritual songs, singing and making melody to the Lord with your heart, giving thanks always and for everything to God the Father in the name of our Lord Jesus Christ.

Ephesians 5:18–20

Psalm 1

Blessed is the man
    who walks not in the counsel of the wicked,
nor stands in the way of sinners,
    nor sits in the seat of scoffers;
but his delight is in the law of the LORD,
    and on His law he meditates day and night.

He is like a tree
    planted by streams of water
that yields its fruit in its season,
    and its leaf does not wither.
In all that he does, he prospers.
The wicked are not so,
    but are like chaff that the wind drives away.

Therefore the wicked will not stand in the
    judgment,
    nor sinners in the congregation of the
    righteous;
for the LORD knows the way of the righteous,
    but the way of the wicked will perish.

Psalm 8

O Lᴏʀᴅ, our Lord,
  how majestic is Your name in all the earth!
You have set Your glory above the heavens.
  Out of the mouth of babies and infants,
You have established strength because of
    Your foes,
    to still the enemy and the avenger.

When I look at Your heavens, the work
    of Your fingers,
  the moon and the stars, which You have
    set in place,
what is man that You are mindful of him,
  and the son of man that You care for him?
Yet You have made him a little lower than
    the heavenly beings
  and crowned him with glory and honor.
You have given him dominion over the
    works of Your hands;
  You have put all things under his feet,
all sheep and oxen,
  and also the beasts of the field,
the birds of the heavens, and the fish of the sea,
  whatever passes along the paths of the seas.

O Lᴏʀᴅ, our Lord,
  how majestic is Your name in all the earth!

Psalm 13

How long, O LORD? Will You forget me
    forever?
    How long will You hide Your face from me?
How long must I take counsel in my soul
    and have sorrow in my heart all the day?
How long shall my enemy be exalted over me?

Consider and answer me, O LORD my God;
    light up my eyes, lest I sleep the sleep of death,
lest my enemy say, "I have prevailed over him,"
    lest my foes rejoice because I am shaken.

But I have trusted in Your steadfast love;
    my heart shall rejoice in Your salvation.
I will sing to the LORD,
    because He has dealt bountifully with me.

Psalm 18:1–3

I love You, O LORD, my strength.
The LORD is my rock and my fortress and
    my deliverer,
    my God, my rock, in whom I take refuge,
    my shield, and the horn of my salvation,
        my stronghold.
    I call upon the LORD, who is worthy to be praised,
    and I am saved from my enemies.

Psalm 23

The LORD is my shepherd; I shall not want.
    He makes me lie down in green pastures.
He leads me beside still waters.
    He restores my soul.
He leads me in paths of righteousness
    for His name's sake.

Even though I walk through the valley of the
    shadow of death,
    I will fear no evil,
for You are with me;
    Your rod and Your staff,
    they comfort me.

You prepare a table before me
    in the presence of my enemies;
You anoint my head with oil;
    my cup overflows.
Surely goodness and mercy shall follow me
    all the days of my life,
and I shall dwell in the house of the LORD
    forever.

Psalm 34:11

Come, O children, listen to me;
I will teach you the fear of the LORD.

Psalm 36:7–8

How precious is Your steadfast love,
    O God!
The children of mankind take refuge in the
    shadow of Your wings.
They feast on the abundance of Your house,
    and You give them drink from the river
    of Your delights.

Psalm 37:23–26

The steps of a man are established by the
    LORD,
    when he delights in His way;
though he fall, he shall not be cast headlong,
    for the LORD upholds his hand.

I have been young, and now am old,
    yet I have not seen the righteous forsaken
    or his children begging for bread.
He is ever lending generously,
    and his children become a blessing.

Have mercy on me, O God,
    according to Your steadfast love;
according to Your abundant mercy
    blot out my transgressions.
Wash me thoroughly from my iniquity,
    and cleanse me from my sin!
For I know my transgressions,
    and my sin is ever before me.
Against You, You only, have I sinned
    and done what is evil in Your sight,
so that You may be justified in Your words
    and blameless in Your judgment.
Behold, I was brought forth in iniquity,
    and in sin did my mother conceive me.
Behold, You delight in truth in the inward
        being,
    and You teach me wisdom in the secret heart.

Purge me with hyssop, and I shall be clean;
    wash me, and I shall be whiter than snow.
Let me hear joy and gladness;
    let the bones that You have broken rejoice.
Hide Your face from my sins,
    and blot out all my iniquities.
Create in me a clean heart, O God,
    and renew a right spirit within me.
Cast me not away from Your presence,

and take not Your Holy Spirit from me.
Restore to me the joy of Your salvation,
    and uphold me with a willing spirit.

Then I will teach transgressors Your ways,
    and sinners will return to You.
Deliver me from bloodguiltiness, O God,
    O God of my salvation,
        and my tongue will sing aloud of Your
        righteousness.
O Lord, open my lips,
    and my mouth will declare Your praise.

Psalm 78:5–7

He established a testimony in Jacob
    and appointed a law in Israel,
which He commanded our fathers
    to teach to their children,
 that the next generation might know them,
    the children yet unborn,
and arise and tell them to their children,
    so that they should set their hope in God
and not forget the works of God,
    but keep His commandments.

Psalm 103:11–13

For as high as the heavens are above the earth,
  so great is His steadfast love toward those
    who fear Him;
as far as the east is from the west,
  so far does He remove our transgressions
    from us.
As a father shows compassion to his children,
  so the LORD shows compassion to those
    who fear Him.

Psalm 103:17–19

The steadfast love of the LORD is from
    everlasting to everlasting on those who
    fear Him,
  and His righteousness to children's children,
to those who keep His covenant
    and remember to do His commandments.
The LORD has established His throne in the
    heavens,
and His kingdom rules over all.

Psalm 113

Praise the LORD!
Praise, O servants of the LORD,
   praise the name of the LORD!

Blessed be the name of the LORD
   from this time forth and forevermore!
From the rising of the sun to its setting,
   the name of the LORD is to be praised!

The LORD is high above all nations,
   and His glory above the heavens!
Who is like the LORD our God,
   who is seated on high,
who looks far down
   on the heavens and the earth?
He raises the poor from the dust
   and lifts the needy from the ash heap,
to make them sit with princes,
   with the princes of His people.
He gives the barren woman a home,
   making her the joyous mother of children.
Praise the LORD!

Psalm 127

Unless the LORD builds the house,
    those who build it labor in vain.
Unless the LORD watches over the city,
    the watchman stays awake in vain.
It is in vain that you rise up early
    and go late to rest,
eating the bread of anxious toil;
    for He gives to His beloved sleep.

Behold, children are a heritage
    from the LORD,
    the fruit of the womb a reward.
Like arrows in the hand of a warrior
    are the children of one's youth.
Blessed is the man
    who fills his quiver with them!
He shall not be put to shame
    when he speaks with his enemies
      in the gate.

Psalm 128

Blessed is everyone who fears the LORD,
    who walks in His ways!
You shall eat the fruit of the labor of your hands;
    you shall be blessed, and it shall be well with
      you.

Your wife will be like a fruitful vine
    within your house;
your children will be like olive shoots
    around your table.
Behold, thus shall the man be blessed
    who fears the LORD.

The LORD bless you from Zion!
    May you see the prosperity of Jerusalem
    all the days of your life!
May you see your children's children!
    Peace be upon Israel!

Psalm 130

Out of the depths I cry to You, O Lord!
    O Lord, hear my voice!
Let Your ears be attentive
    to the voice of my pleas for mercy!
If You, O Lord, should mark iniquities,
    O Lord, who could stand?
But with You there is forgiveness,
    that You may be feared.

I wait for the Lord, my soul waits,
    and in His word I hope;
my soul waits for the Lord
    more than watchmen for the morning,

more than watchmen for the morning.

O Israel, hope in the LORD!
    For with the LORD there is steadfast love,
    and with Him is plentiful redemption.
And He will redeem Israel
    from all his iniquities.

Psalm 138:7–8

Though I walk in the midst of trouble,
    You preserve my life;
You stretch out Your hand against the
    wrath of my enemies,
    and Your right hand delivers me.
The LORD will fulfill His purpose for me;
    Your steadfast love, O LORD, endures forever.
    Do not forsake the work of Your hands.

Psalm 145:1–7

I will extol You, my God and King,
    and bless Your name forever and ever.
Every day I will bless You
    and praise Your name forever and ever.
Great is the LORD, and greatly to be praised,
    and His greatness is unsearchable.

One generation shall commend Your works
    to another,
  and shall declare Your mighty acts.
On the glorious splendor of Your majesty,
  and on Your wondrous works, I will meditate.
They shall speak of the might of Your
    awesome deeds,
  and I will declare Your greatness.
They shall pour forth the fame of Your
    abundant goodness
  and shall sing aloud of Your righteousness.

Psalm 147:1–6

Praise the LORD!
For it is good to sing praises to our God;
  for it is pleasant, and a song of praise
    is fitting.
The LORD builds up Jerusalem;
  He gathers the outcasts of Israel.
He heals the brokenhearted
  and binds up their wounds.
He determines the number of the stars;
  He gives to all of them their names.
Great is our Lord, and abundant in power;
  His understanding is beyond measure.
The LORD lifts up the humble;
  He casts the wicked to the ground.

Psalm 149

Praise the LORD!
Sing to the LORD a new song,
   His praise in the assembly of the godly!
Let Israel be glad in his Maker;
   let the children of Zion rejoice in their King!
Let them praise His name with dancing,
   making melody to Him with tambourine
     and lyre!
For the LORD takes pleasure in His people;
   He adorns the humble with salvation.
Let the godly exult in glory;
   let them sing for joy on their beds.
Let the high praises of God be in their throats
   and two-edged swords in their hands,
to execute vengeance on the nations
   and punishments on the peoples,
to bind their kings with chains
   and their nobles with fetters of iron,
to execute on them the judgment written!
   This is honor for all His godly ones.
Praise the LORD!

My Family's Favorite Psalms

_____

_____

_____

_____

_____

_____

_____

_____

My Family's Favorite Psalms

SCRIPTURE TEXTS

All Scripture is breathed out by God and profitable for teaching, for reproof, for correction, and for training in righteousness, that the man of God may be complete, equipped for every good work.

2 Timothy 3:16–17

Deuteronomy 6:6–8

And these words that I command you today shall be on your heart. You shall teach them diligently to your children, and shall talk of them when you sit in your house, and when you walk by the way, and when you lie down, and when you rise. You shall bind them as a sign on your hand, and they shall be as frontlets between your eyes.

Proverbs 3:5–6

Trust in the LORD with all your heart, and
do not lean on your own
    understanding.
In all your ways acknowledge Him,
    and He will make straight your paths.

Proverbs 14:25–27

A truthful witness saves lives, but one who breathes out lies is deceitful. In the fear of the Lord one has strong confidence, and his children will have a refuge. The fear of the Lord is a fountain of life, that one may turn away from the snares of death.

Proverbs 20:6–8

Many a man proclaims his own steadfast love, but a faithful man who can find? The righteous who walks in his integrity—blessed are his children after him! A king who sits on the throne of judgment winnows all evil with his eyes.

Proverbs 22:6

Train up a child in the way he should go; even when he is old he will not depart from it.

Proverbs 31:10–12, 26–31

An excellent wife who can find? She is far more precious than jewels. The heart of her husband trusts in her, and he will have no lack of gain. She does him good, and not harm, all the days of her life. . . . She opens her mouth with wisdom, and the teaching of kindness is on her tongue. She looks well to the ways of her household and does not eat the bread of idleness. Her children rise up and call her blessed;

her husband also, and he praises her: "Many women have done excellently, but you surpass them all." Charm is deceitful, and beauty is vain, but a woman who fears the Lord is to be praised. Give her of the fruit of her hands, and let her works praise her in the gates.

Isaiah 54:1–10

"Sing, O barren one, who did not bear;
    break forth into singing and cry aloud,
    you who have not been in labor!
For the children of the desolate one
    will be more
    than the children of her who is
    married," says the Lord.
"Enlarge the place of your tent,
    and let the curtains of your habitations
    be stretched out;
do not hold back; lengthen your cords
    and strengthen your stakes.
For you will spread abroad to the right
    and to the left,
    and your offspring will possess the
    nations

and will people the desolate cities.
"Fear not, for you will not be ashamed;
    be not confounded, for you will not be
        disgraced;
for you will forget the shame of your
        youth,
    and the reproach of your widowhood
    you will remember no more.
For your Maker is your husband,
    the Lord of hosts is His name;
and the Holy One of Israel is your
        Redeemer,
    the God of the whole earth He is
        called.
For the Lord has called you
    like a wife deserted and grieved in
        spirit,
like a wife of youth when she is cast off,
    says your God.
For a brief moment I deserted you,
    but with great compassion I will gather
        you.
In overflowing anger for a moment
    I hid My face from you,

but with everlasting love I will have

compassion on you,"

says the LORD, your Redeemer.

"This is like the days of Noah to Me:

as I swore that the waters of Noah

should no more go over the earth,

so I have sworn that I will not be angry

with you,

and will not rebuke you.

For the mountains may depart

and the hills be removed,

but My steadfast love shall not depart

from you,

and My covenant of peace shall not be

removed,"

says the LORD, who has compassion on

you.

Isaiah 59:21

"And as for Me, this is My covenant with them," says the LORD: "My Spirit that is upon you, and My words that I have put in your mouth, shall not depart out of your mouth, or out of the mouth of your offspring, or out of the mouth of your children's offspring," says the LORD, "from this time forth and forevermore."

Isaiah 63:7–9

I will recount the steadfast love of the
    LORD,
    the praises of the LORD,
according to all that the LORD has granted
    us,
    and the great goodness to the house
    of Israel
that He has granted them according to His
    compassion,
    according to the abundance of His
    steadfast love.
For He said, "Surely they are My people,

children who will not deal falsely."
And He became their Savior.
In all their affliction He was afflicted,
    and the angel of His presence saved
        them;
in His love and in his pity He redeemed
        them;
He lifted them up and carried them all
        the days of old.

Jeremiah 29:11

For I know the plans I have for you, declares the LORD, plans for welfare and not for evil, to give you a future and a hope.

Matthew 11:25–30

At that time Jesus declared, "I thank You, Father, Lord of heaven and earth, that You have hidden these things from the wise and understanding and revealed them to little children; yes, Father, for such was Your gracious will. All things have been handed over to Me by My Father, and no one knows the Son except the

Father, and no one knows the Father except the Son and anyone to whom the Son chooses to reveal Him. Come to Me, all who labor and are heavy laden, and I will give you rest. Take My yoke upon you, and learn from Me, for I am gentle and lowly in heart, and you will find rest for your souls. For My yoke is easy, and My burden is light."

Matthew 18:2–4

And calling to Him a child, He put him in the midst of them and said, "Truly, I say to you, unless you turn and become like children, you will never enter the kingdom of heaven. Whoever humbles himself like this child is the greatest in the kingdom of heaven.

Matthew 19:13–15

Then children were brought to Him that He might lay His hands on them and pray. The disciples rebuked the people, but Jesus said, "Let the little children come to Me and do not hinder them, for to such belongs the kingdom of heaven." And He laid His hands on them and went away.

Matthew 23:37–39

O Jerusalem, Jerusalem, the city that kills the prophets and stones those who are sent to it! How often would I have gathered your children together as a hen gathers her brood under her wings, and you were not willing! See, your house is left to you desolate. For I tell you, you will not see Me again, until you say, "Blessed is He who comes in the name of the Lord."

Mark 10:29–30

Jesus said, "Truly, I say to you, there is no one who has left house or brothers or sisters or mother or father or children or lands, for My sake and for the gospel, who will not receive a hundredfold now in this time, houses and brothers and sisters and mothers and children and lands, with persecutions, and in the age to come eternal life."

Luke 11:9–12

And I tell you, ask, and it will be given to you; seek, and you will find; knock, and it will be opened to you. For everyone who asks receives, and the one who seeks finds, and to the one who knocks it will be opened. What father among you, if his son asks for a fish, will instead of a fish give him a serpent; or if he asks for an egg, will give him a scorpion? If you then, who are evil, know how to give good gifts to your children, how much more will the heavenly Father give the Holy Spirit to those who ask Him!

John 1:11–13

He came to His own, and His own people did not receive Him. But to all who did receive Him, who believed in His name, He gave the right to become children of God, who were born, not of blood nor of the will of the flesh nor of the will of man, but of God.

Acts 2:38–40

And Peter said to them, "Repent and be baptized every one of you in the name of Jesus Christ for the forgiveness of your sins, and you will receive the gift of the Holy Spirit. For the promise is for you and for your children and for all who are far off, everyone whom the Lord our God calls to Himself." And with many other words he bore witness and continued to exhort them, saying, "Save yourselves from this crooked generation."

Romans 8:15–17

For you did not receive the spirit of slavery to fall back into fear, but you have received the Spirit of adoption as sons, by whom we cry, "Abba! Father!" The Spirit Himself bears witness with our spirit that we are children of God, and if children, then heirs—heirs of God and fellow heirs with Christ, provided we suffer with Him in order that we may also be glorified with Him.

Ephesians 6:1–4

Children, obey your parents in the Lord, for this is right. "Honor your father and mother" (this is the first commandment with a promise), "that it may go well with you and that you may live long in the land." Fathers, do not provoke your children to anger, but bring them up in the discipline and instruction of the Lord.

1 Thessalonians 5:4–6

But you are not in darkness, brothers, for that day to surprise you like a thief. For you are all children of light, children of the day. We are not of the night or of the darkness. So then let us not sleep, as others do, but let us keep awake and be sober.

1 John 2:12–14

I am writing to you, little children,
    because your sins are forgiven for His
        name's sake.
I am writing to you, fathers,

because you know Him who is from
the beginning.
I am writing to you, young men,
because you have overcome the evil
one.
I write to you, children,
because you know the Father.
I write to you, fathers,
because you know Him who is from
the beginning.
I write to you, young men,
because you are strong,
and the word of God abides in you,
and you have overcome the evil one.

1 John 3:1–3

See what kind of love the Father has given to us, that we should be called children of God; and so we are. The reason why the world does not know us is that it did not know Him. Beloved, we are God's children now, and what we will be has not yet appeared; but we know that when He appears we shall be like Him, because we shall see Him as He is. And everyone who thus hopes in Him purifies Himself as He is pure.

3 John 3–5

For I rejoiced greatly when the brothers came and testified to your truth, as indeed you are walking in the truth. I have no greater joy than to hear that my children are walking in the truth. Beloved, it is a faithful thing you do in all your efforts for these brothers, strangers as they are, who testified to your love before the church. You will do well to send them on their journey in a manner worthy of God.

Revelation 3:10–11

Because you have kept My word about patient endurance, I will keep you from the hour of trial that is coming on the whole world, to try those who dwell on the earth. I am coming soon. Hold fast what you have, so that no one may seize your crown.

My Family's
Favorite Bible Verses

_____

_____

_____

_____

_____

_____

_____

_____

_____

My Family's
Favorite Bible Verses

PRAYERS

Rejoice always, pray without ceasing, give thanks in all circumstances; for this is the will of God in Christ Jesus for you.

1 Thessalonians 5:16–18

GENERAL PRAYERS

And this is the confidence that we have toward Him, that if we ask anything according to His will He hears us. And if we know that He hears us in whatever we ask, we know that we have the requests that we have asked of Him.

1 John 5:14–15

The Lord's Prayer

Our Father who art in heaven,
   hallowed be Thy name,
   Thy kingdom come,
   Thy will be done on earth
      as it is in heaven;
   give us this day our daily bread;
   and forgive us our trespasses
      as we forgive those
      who trespass against us;
and lead us not into temptation,
but deliver us from evil.
For Thine is the kingdom
   and the power and the glory
   forever and ever. Amen.

Luther's Morning Prayer

I thank You, my heavenly Father, through Jesus Christ, Your dear Son, that You have kept me this night from all harm and danger; and I pray that You would keep me this day also from sin and every evil, that all my doings and life may please You. For into Your hands I com-

mend myself, my body and soul, and all things.
Let Your holy angel be with me, that the evil
foe may have no power over me. Amen.

Midday Prayer

Lord of faithfulness, keep me focused on
my tasks for the day. Grant me strength as
the burdens of the day threaten to distract me
from my callings. As Jesus took time for prayer
with You, help me to stop in the toils of life for
moments of conversation with You. Use these
times to equip me better to serve You and others as I begin again the work You have given
me. Keep me from grumbling about my du-
ties—that they are too mundane, too difficult,
too humble, too frustrating, too small. Remind
me that You use us all for Your glory and the
benefit of others. Help me to wisely use the
gifts You have given me to serve You. In Your
Son's name I pray. Amen.   *(Portals of Prayer)*

Luther's Evening Prayer

I thank You, my heavenly Father, through Jesus Christ, Your dear Son, that You have graciously kept me this day; and I pray that You would forgive me all my sins where I have done wrong, and graciously keep me this night. For into Your hands I commend myself, my body and soul, and all things. Let Your holy angel be with me, that the evil foe may have no power over me. Amen.

Sunday

Lord of all, You promise Your constant presence. This is especially evident as I enter Your house to worship. Whether this morning or another time, let me do so with thanksgiving and a willing spirit. Clean my heart and prepare it to serve You throughout the coming week. Heal my relationship with You through Your words of forgiveness. Bring me closer to others as I share this time with fellow believers. Help me remember that I join with more than those I see today. I join with all saints on earth, all saints in You, and all heavenly beings. Guard and protect all who gather today, and let their witness to Your glory shine as a light to those still in darkness. Amen. *(Portals of Prayer)*

Monday

Lord of righteousness, a new week of service to You begins. With it, I have excitement, fear, happiness, and grumblings. Have mercy on my hesitations, and enable me to meet the challenges of the coming days with a heart of courage. Forgive my doubts, and give me eyes of wisdom to see Your will in my goings-on. Be gracious to me in my failings, and as I reach out to others in my life, let me do so with a mouth of patience. Lord, look on all who begin this day in so many different situations and emotions. Assure them all that they are in Your care. Help me share this truth with others. In Jesus' name I pray. Amen. *(Portals of Prayer)*

Tuesday

Lord, help me find joy in all I do today as I serve You in the ways You have planned for me. Help me to show love to all people so that through my actions, I may reflect the love You have for me and for all others. Even during times that test my ability to show love, remind me of Your unconditional love and forgiveness. Forgive my sinful acts and the acts I neglect today. Use me as Your instrument in sharing Your love to the world, whether it be to one small child or to hundreds of people today. Remind me that no task is too small and that joy can be found in even the simplest gestures. In Jesus' name I pray. Amen.

Wednesday

God of peace, remind me that Your peace passes all understanding. A peaceful life does not mean one without any struggles or strife. Instead, You give a peace not as the world gives, but an eternal peace even in the midst of difficult times. Grant me this peace today, and help me share it with others. Help me to be patient with whatever comes my way today, even circumstances that test me and cause me frustration. Show me ways to help others so that I do not test their patience but rather increase the peace they have in You. In the name of my Savior, who was patient unto death, I pray. Amen.

Thursday

Good and gracious Lord, Your kindness is evident with each passing day. With the daily bread You provide, I taste and see that You are good. In Your goodness to others, use me today to serve in Your kingdom. Enable me to show kindness to others so that they may know of Your good will through my words and deeds. Thank You for all the goodness and kindness You show me daily; forgive me when I take all You do for granted. Help me model thankfulness to my family so that they, too, remember Your care for them. In Jesus' name I pray. Amen.

Friday

Faithful Father, You never forsake me. Forgive me for the times I've ignored the needs of my own children and for the times I've ignored Your paternal love. Strengthen me to be a faithful servant as I care for the children You have given me. Equip me to be faithful to You so that my children can learn by my example how to live faithful lives of service. As You lead and serve, guide me to lead and serve so that my children will do the same for those around them. Give me joy in my love for You so my family can see that the Christian life is not one of obligation but of thankful response to Your unfailing love and faithfulness. In Your Son's name I pray. Amen.

Saturday

Almighty God, You are the Creator of the world. Even so, Your gentleness brings comfort to those who marvel at Your power. You are in control of all, and yet You choose to show mercy and love to Your lowly people. There are times when I abuse the authority I have over others and turn loved ones away with my uncaring words. Help me to show gentleness to those I love so that they can approach me with their needs. When all seems out of control, give me self-control to handle each situation with grace and with the knowledge that You are ultimately in control of all things. In Jesus' name I pray. Amen.

TOPICAL PRAYERS

For this reason I bow my knees before the Father, . . . [that] He may grant you to be strengthened with power through His Spirit in your inner being, so that Christ may dwell in your hearts through faith.

Ephesians 3:14–17

A General Prayer of Thanksgiving

Heavenly Father, You care for us as Your children. You give us what we need, even when we don't ask. Your wisdom far surpasses our own, and You care for us in ways we could never imagine. At times, we don't recognize or even want Your good gifts. Forgive our ingratitude and fill us with joyful thanks, especially for the most surprising gift of all: salvation through Your Son, in whose name we pray. Amen.

(Portals of Prayer)

Longing for a Child

Dear Lord, Hannah prayed that You would "look on the affliction of Your servant and remember me and not forget your servant" (1 Samuel 1:11). O God, we are afflicted with grief and longing. We sometimes feel forgotten. We ask that You give us strength and patience during this time of trial. We also ask that You hear our plea and grant us our desire for a child. Forgive us for not trusting Your ways, O Lord, and keep us mindful of Your promises.

Reassure us of Your love. According to Your loving will, grant us the joy of a child. Grant us peace as we wait. Amen.

Waiting for an Adoption

Dear loving Father, You have adopted us as Your own children, and You love us with unconditional love. We long to share that love with our adopted child, and we can hardly wait for the day *he/she* is in our arms. Grant us patience as we prepare for this new addition to our family. Keep our child safe in Your hands, and nurture *him/her* in Your care. Bless the birth parents and those who care for our child while we wait. Give us the gifts we need to be parents as we bring up our child in the knowledge of You, our Father, and of Jesus, our Savior and Brother. Amen.

Waiting during Pregnancy

Creator of all, You have begun a new life, and You are knitting this child together as we watch in wonder. Guard and protect this little one as *he/she* grows every day. Give us patience as we wait, and encourage us as we already care for one of Your precious children. Ease our worries, and keep mother and baby safe on this incredible journey of pregnancy. Preserve us all, and remind us of Your unfailing love. Amen.

At the Birth of a Child

Almighty God, creator of all that exists, we thank You this day for the birth of *name*. As you have added *him/her* to the human family, so also unite *him/her* to Your Holy Church through the waters of Holy Baptism. By the gracious working of Your Holy Spirit, help *him/her* to grow in Your nurture and admonition that *he/she* may bring glory to You and serve others in Your name; through Jesus Christ, our Lord. Amen. *(LSB, p. 318)*

Life as a Baptized Child of God

Merciful Father, through Holy Baptism You called us to be Your own possession. Grant that our lives may evidence the working of Your Holy Spirit in love, joy, peace, patience, kindness, goodness, faithfulness, gentleness, and self-control, according to the image of Your only-begotten Son, Jesus Christ, our Savior. Amen. (*LSB*, p. 310)

Anniversary of a Baptism

Gracious Lord, we give thanks that in Holy Baptism we receive forgiveness of sins, deliverance from death and the devil, and eternal salvation. On this baptismal anniversary, bless *name* continually by Your Word and Spirit that *he/she* may faithfully keep the covenant into which *he/she* has been called, boldly confess *his/her* Savior, and finally share with all Your saints the joys of eternal life; through Jesus Christ, our Lord. Amen. (*LSB*, p. 310)

For Blessing on the Word

Lord God, bless Your Word wherever it is proclaimed. Make it a word of power and peace to convert those not yet Your own and to

confirm those who have come to saving faith.
May Your Word pass from the ear to the heart,
from the heart to the lip, and from the lip to
the life that, as You have promised, Your Word
may achieve the purpose for which You send it;
through Jesus Christ, my Lord. Amen.

(*LSB, Prayers for Worship*)

Grace to Receive the Word

Blessed Lord, You have caused all Holy
Scriptures to be written for our learning. Grant
that we may so hear them, read, mark, learn,
and inwardly digest them that, by patience and
comfort of Your holy Word, we may embrace
and ever hold fast the blessed hope of everlasting life; through Jesus Christ, our Lord. Amen.

(*LSB*, p. 308)

For Home and Family

Visit, O Lord, the homes in which Your
people dwell, and keep all harm and danger
far from them. Grant that we may dwell to-

gether in peace under the protection of Your holy angels, sharing eternally in Your blessings; through Jesus Christ, our Lord. Amen. *(LSB, p. 315)*

Care of Children

Almighty God, heavenly Father, You have blessed us with the joy and care of children. Give us calm strength and patient wisdom that, as they grow in years, we may teach them to love whatever is just and true and good, following the example of our Savior, Jesus Christ, our Lord. Amen. *(LSB, p. 315)*

Care for a Difficult Child

Lord God, You called the Israelites Your stubborn and rebellious children. I am just as stubborn and rebellious as they were. And now, I see from Your perspective how hurtful it can be. Forgive me, Lord, for the times I have disregarded Your will for my life and followed my own sinful desires. Lord, I need Your help as I care for my child. Give me the patience You have for me. Enable me to speak Your truth in love. It can be difficult to show my child the Law of what we should do and the Gospel of what You have done for us. Give me wisdom so that my words are true and clear and patient and loving. Uplift me when I am exhausted with this difficult task, and comfort me with Your forgiveness and love. Amen.

Care for an Ailing Child

Father in heaven, I cannot imagine the pain You felt when You saw Your Son in agony on the cross. I cannot imagine the sorrow You feel when You see any one of Your children suffering. It hurts me to see my child in need, and I feel helpless to make things right. O Lord, have mercy on *name*, and restore *him/her* to health. Give me strength to care for *him/her*, and enable me to comfort *him/her*. Whatever Your will may be for the future, I know my child is in Your hands, and I know that I am too. Give me the peace that passes all understanding, and help me reflect Your love to my child so that *he/she* knows that *he/she* is safe in Your care. In my Savior's name I pray. Amen.

Care for Young Children

Lord of Love, Your patience knows no bounds. My own falters daily. Thank You for this precious child, who brings so much joy to my life. This child brings much testing as well. Sometimes, this dear one needs me every moment. Other times, it is as if my efforts don't matter at all. When my attempts to soothe my little one fail, when constant care leaves me physically and emotionally exhausted, when I don't seem to do anything right, come to my aid. Forgive my impatience. Give me strength. Help me show the love Jesus had when He beckoned the little children to Him. Remind me that I, too, am Your child, whom You love dearly. In Jesus' name I pray. Amen.

Care for Grade School Children

Dear God, people are always reminding me that time goes by quickly when watching children grow up. I can already see it happening, but I'm so often distracted by the homework and hobbies and sports that come with this phase of life. Other times, I feel so bogged down with the repetition of each week that I forget to be thankful for my children. Forgive me for my shortsightedness. Give me strength during the demanding schedules. Remind me to make room for the important to-do task of spending time with my family as well as with You. Help me see what I'm teaching my children with my words and actions. Guide me to guide my family in Your ways. When I fail, forgive me and remind me of Your never-ending love. Help me to show that love to my family. In Jesus' name I pray. Amen.

Care for Teenage Children

Caring Father, You have seen generation after generation grow and mature. You know the sins that plague our world better than I do. As my children are gaining independence and responsibility, preserve them from harm and danger. Equip them with Your Spirit, that they may be witnesses of You as they live their lives more and more without my direct presence.

You are always with them; help me to trust in You. Give us all patience and wisdom as we learn our new roles. Help us all know the right balance of authority, freedom, and responsibility. Keep my children steadfast in Your Word so that You may guide them now and throughout their lives, as You have from the beginning.

Care for Adult Children

Dear God, our children have grown into adulthood, but we are still parents who love them dearly. Help us all in our new roles. Give discernment to our children, and guide them in Your ways, which they have learned throughout their lives. Keep them firmly in Your hand, and use them to reach out to others, including children of their own, with Your love. Remind us that it is Your will for children to leave their father and their mother to begin new families. Give us wisdom as to when we should reach out to our children and when we should be content to watch them make decisions of their own. Help us to be good models of Christian adults so that our teaching—though different—can benefit our children even today. In Jesus' name we pray. Amen.

Vocation

Lord, You call each of us to serve You in many ways. Spouse, parent, sibling, child, friend, volunteer, employee, employer, the list is extensive. Thank You for using us to Your purpose. Forgive us when we scorn the tasks that we deem too lowly. Help us when we fear the tasks that seem too daunting. Enable us to find joy in the roles You have given us, and equip us to do them well to Your glory. Thank You for Your Son's most important calling: to save us from sin and death. Help us to respond in love toward others. In Jesus' name we pray. Amen.

Proper Use of Leisure

O God, give us times of refreshment and peace in the course of this busy life. Grant that we may so use our leisure to rebuild our bodies and renew our minds that we may be opened

to the goodness of Your creation; through Jesus
Christ, our Lord. Amen. (LSB, p. 311)

Times of Celebration

God of glory, thank You for this time of joy!
Thank You for the gifts You have given to this
family, and help us to give You the praise and
glory for this celebration. Bless this time as we
rejoice in Your name, and lead us to savor these
happy memories. Let all who see us rejoicing
know that You are the giver of all good things.
In Jesus' name we pray. Amen.

Times of Parting

God of families, You desire a relationship
with us, and You nurture our relationships
with one another. When the time comes for
us to part from our children, the pain can be
deep and the grief can be intense. Protect our
kids, Lord, and keep them in Your care, as You
have since the day You formed them. Give us,
the parents, strength and wisdom as we trust
You. Let us enjoy every day You give and every
phase of life as we await a joyful reunion with

the ones we love. In Your Son's name we pray. Amen.

During Tragedy

God of wisdom, I simply cannot understand how deeply sin has affected our lives. Right now, I can only stare at the world through tears and wonder how I can go on. I call out to You, my Lord, for endurance. Help me share this strength with my family and those around me. When my words fail, Lord, wrap me in Your love and remind me of Your healing hand. When I fall to my knees, uplift me with Your promises and comfort me with Your Word. Even when I don't know how to feel, assure me that You are always with me. In time, help me heal and show others the certain hope I have in You because of Jesus, my Savior. Amen.

For the Sick

Lord of healing, it pains me to see my loved ones sick. It pains You too. In this fallen world, disease and suffering sadden us all. Just as You healed Naaman and so many others, please also heal those in our lives who ail. Grant comfort and the peace that only You can give, no matter what happens. We pray in Jesus' name and according to Your good and gracious will. Amen.

(Portals of Prayer)

By the Bereaved

Loving Father, this loss is so painful. I know You, too, feel the sadness that death brings— sadness that was not meant for us. Please comfort me with the peace that only You can give, the patience it takes to grieve, and the certain hope of Jesus' resurrection. Help me remember that departed saints worship together with us in praise to You. Remind me that You will reunite all Your people on the Last Day. I pray in Jesus' name. Amen.

(Portals of Prayer)

For Deliverance from Sin

Holy Lord God, sin and evil pervade every day. My own failings and mistakes are evidence that I need Your rescue and continual forgiveness. Lord, guide me through this place of hardship, and enable me to act according to Your will. Strengthen Your people until the Last Day, when sin is conquered forever and the trouble of this world is destroyed. I ask this in the name of Jesus Christ, my Savior. Amen.

(Portals of Prayer)

For Patience While Recovering

God Almighty, Scripture records that You have shown the power of Your healing hand to so many who were sick or hurting. But even in the midst of miracles, many endured hardship for a long time. Jesus knows what it is like to suffer more than any other. In my own struggles, remind me that You care. Grant me patience as I recover, that even in waiting, I can witness to Your love. Amen.

For Help in Time of Temptation

God of strength, temptation surrounds me to the point that it is difficult to see anything else. Yet, You promise that You will never allow me to be tempted beyond what I can bear. Grant that I will cry out to You for hope when enticement is all I see. Comfort me with the truth that Jesus, too, faced temptation. He knows this struggle. But Jesus overcame temptation and paid for all sin, including my own. Amen.

My Family's
Favorite Prayers

_____

_____

_____

_____

_____

_____

_____

_____

_____

My Family's
Favorite Prayers

_____

_____

_____

_____

_____

_____

_____

_____

_____

_____

Hymns

Let the word of Christ dwell in you richly, teaching and admonishing one another in all wisdom, singing psalms and hymns and spiritual songs, with thankfulness in your hearts to God. *Colossians 3:16*

God Loves Me Dearly

God loves me dearly,
Grants me salvation,
God loves me dearly,
Loves even me.

Refrain: Therefore I'll say again:
God loves me dearly,
God loves me dearly,
Loves even me.

I was in slav'ry,
Sin, death, and darkness;
God's love was working
To make me free. *Refrain*

He sent forth Jesus,
My dear Redeemer,
He sent forth Jesus
And set me free. *Refrain*
Jesus, my Savior,
Himself did offer;

Jesus, my Savior,
Paid all I owed. *Refrain*

Now I will praise You,
O Love Eternal;
Now I will praise You
All my life long. *Refrain*
(LSB 392)

All Who Believe and Are Baptized

All who believe and are baptized
   Shall see the Lord's salvation;
Baptized into the death of Christ,
   They are a new creation.
Through Christ's redemption they shall
     stand
Among the glorious, heav'nly band
   Of ev'ry tribe and nation.

With one accord, O God, we pray:
   Grant us Your Holy Spirit.
Help us in our infirmity
   Through Jesus' blood and merit.

Grant us to grow in grace each day
That by this sacrament we may
   Eternal life inherit.
(*LSB* 601)

Lord, Keep Us Steadfast in Your Word

Lord, keep us steadfast in Your Word;
Curb those who by deceit or sword
Would wrest the kingdom from Your Son
And bring to naught all He has done.

Lord Jesus Christ, Your pow'r make
   known,
For You are Lord of lords alone;
Defend Your holy Church that we
May sing Your praise eternally.

O Comforter of priceless worth,
Send peace and unity on earth;
Support us in our final strife
And lead us out of death to life.
(*LSB* 655)

Let Us Ever Walk with Jesus

Let us ever walk with Jesus,
   Follow His example pure,
Through a world that would deceive us
   And to sin our spirits lure.
Onward in His footsteps treading,
   Pilgrims here, our home above,
   Full of faith and hope and love,
Let us do the Father's bidding.
   Faithful Lord, with me abide;
   I shall follow where You guide.

Let us suffer here with Jesus
   And with patience bear our cross.
Joy will follow all our sadness;
   Where He is, there is no loss.
Though today we sow no laughter,
   We shall reap celestial joy;
All discomforts that annoy
   Shall give way to mirth hereafter.
Jesus, here I share Your woe;
   Help me there Your joy to know.

Let us gladly die with Jesus.
    Since by death He conquered death,
He will free us from destruction,
    Give to us immortal breath.
Let us mortify all passion
    That would lead us into sin;
And the grave that shuts us in
    Shall but prove the gate to heaven.
Jesus, here with You I die,
    There to live with You on high.

Let us also live with Jesus.
    He has risen from the dead
That to life we may awaken.
    Jesus, You are now our head.
We are Your own living members;
    Where You live, there we shall be
In Your presence constantly,
    Living there with You forever.
Jesus, let me faithful be,
    Life eternal grant to me.

(*LSB* 685; text: © 1978 *Lutheran Book of Worship*)

Savior, like a Shepherd Lead Us

Savior, like a shepherd lead us;
    Much we need Your tender care.
In Your pleasant pastures feed us,
    For our use Your fold prepare.
Blessèd Jesus, blessèd Jesus,
    You have bought us; we are Yours.
Blessèd Jesus, blessèd Jesus,
    You have bought us; we are Yours.

We are Yours; in love befriend us,
    Be the guardian of our way;
Keep Your flock, from sin defend us,
    Seek us when we go astray.
Blessèd Jesus, blessèd Jesus,
    Hear us children when we pray.
Blessèd Jesus, blessèd Jesus,
    Hear us children when we pray.

You have promised to receive us,
    Poor and sinful though we be;
You have mercy to relieve us,
    Grace to cleanse, and pow'r to free.

Blessèd Jesus, blessèd Jesus,
　　Early let us turn to You.
Blessèd Jesus, blessèd Jesus,
　　Early let us turn to You.

Early let us seek Your favor,
　　Early let us do Your will;
Blessèd Lord and only Savior,
　　With Your love our spirits fill.
Blessèd Jesus, blessèd Jesus,
　　You have loved us, love us still.
Blessèd Jesus, blessèd Jesus,
　　You have loved us, love us still.

(*LSB* 711)

I Am Trusting Thee, Lord Jesus

I am trusting Thee, Lord Jesus,
　　Trusting only Thee;
Trusting Thee for full salvation,
　　Great and free.

I am trusting Thee for pardon;
　　At Thy feet I bow,

For Thy grace and tender mercy
   Trusting now.

I am trusting Thee for cleansing
   In the crimson flood;
Trusting Thee to make me holy
   By Thy blood.

I am trusting Thee to guide me;
   Thou alone shalt lead,
Ev'ry day and hour supplying
   All my need.

I am trusting Thee for power;
   Thine can never fail.
Words which Thou Thyself shalt give me
   Must prevail.

I am trusting Thee, Lord Jesus;
   Never let me fall.
I am trusting Thee forever
   And for all.

(*LSB* 729)

O God, Forsake Me Not

O God, forsake me not!
  Your gracious presence lend me;
Lord, lead Your helpless child;
  Your Holy Spirit send me
That I my course may run.
  O be my light, my lot,
My staff, my rock, my shield—
  O God, forsake me not!

O God, forsake me not!
  Take not Your Spirit from me;
Do not permit the might
  Of sin to overcome me.
Increase my feeble faith,
  Which You alone have wrought.
O be my strength and pow'r—
  O God, forsake me not!

O God, forsake me not!
  Lord, hear my supplication!
In ev'ry evil hour
  Help me resist temptation;

And when the prince of hell
   My conscience seeks to blot,
Be then not far from me—
   O God, forsake me not!

O God, forsake me not!
   Lord, I am Yours forever.
O keep me strong in faith
   That I may leave You never.
Grant me a blessèd end
   When my good fight is fought;
Help me in life and death—
   O God, forsake me not!

(*LSB* 731)

Amazing Grace

Amazing grace—how sweet the sound—
   That saved a wretch like me!
I once was lost but now am found,
   Was blind but now I see!

The Lord has promised good to me,
   His Word my hope secures;
He will my shield and portion be

As long as life endures.

Through many dangers, toils, and snares
    I have already come;
His grace has brought me safe thus far,
    His grace will lead me home.

Yes, when this flesh and heart shall fail
    And mortal life shall cease,
Amazing grace shall then prevail
    In heaven's joy and peace.

When we've been there ten thousand
years,
    Bright shining as the sun,
We've no less days to sing God's praise
    Than when we'd first begun.

(*LSB* 744)

What a Friend We Have in Jesus

What a friend we have in Jesus,
    All our sins and griefs to bear!
What a privilege to carry

Ev'rything to God in prayer!
Oh, what peace we often forfeit;
   Oh, what needless pain we bear—
All because we do not carry
   Ev'rything to God in prayer!

Have we trials and temptations?
   Is there trouble anywhere?
We should never be discouraged—
   Take it to the Lord in prayer.
Can we find a friend so faithful
   Who will all our sorrows share?
Jesus knows our ev'ry weakness—
   Take it to the Lord in prayer.

Are we weak and heavy laden,
   Cumbered with a load of care?
Precious Savior, still our refuge—
   Take it to the Lord in prayer.
Do thy friends despise, forsake thee?
   Take it to the Lord in prayer.
In His arms He'll take and shield thee;
   Thou wilt find a solace there.

(LSB 770)

Take My Life and Let It Be

Take my life and let it be
Consecrated, Lord, to Thee;
Take my moments and my days,
Let them flow in ceaseless praise.

Take my hands and let them move
At the impulse of Thy love;
Take my feet and let them be
Swift and beautiful for Thee.

Take my voice and let me sing
Always, only for my King;
Take my lips and let them be
Filled with messages from Thee.

Take my silver and my gold,
Not a mite would I withhold;
Take my intellect and use
Ev'ry pow'r as Thou shalt choose.

Take my will and make it Thine,
It shall be no longer mine;

Take my heart, it is Thine own,
It shall be Thy royal throne.

Take my love, my Lord, I pour
At Thy feet its treasure store;
Take myself, and I will be
Ever, only, all for Thee.
(*LSB* 783)

O God of God, O Light of Light

O God of God, O Light of Light,
 O Prince of Peace and King of kings:
To You in heaven's glory bright
 The song of praise forever rings.
To Him who sits upon the throne,
 The Lamb once slain but raised again,
Be all the glory He has won,
 All thanks and praise! Amen, amen.

For deep in prophets' sacred page,
 And grand in poets' wingèd word,
Slowly in type, from age to age
 The nations saw their coming Lord;

Till through the deep Judean night
    Rang out the song, "Goodwill to men!"
Sung once by firstborn sons of light,
    It echoes now, "Goodwill!" Amen.

That life of truth, those deeds of love,
    That death so steeped in hate and
scorn—
These all are past, and now above
    He reigns, our King once crowned with
thorn.
Lift up your heads, O mighty gates!
    So sang that host beyond our ken.
Lift up your heads, your King awaits.
    We lift them up. Amen, amen.

Then raise to Christ a mighty song,
    And shout His name, His mercies tell!
Sing, heav'nly host, your praise prolong,
    And all on earth, your anthem swell!
All hail, O Lamb for sinners slain!
    Forever let the song ascend!
Worthy the Lamb, enthroned to reign,
    All glory, pow'r! Amen, amen.

(*LSB* 810)

Hark, the Voice of Jesus Crying

Hark, the voice of Jesus crying,
    "Who will go and work today?
Fields are white and harvests waiting—
    Who will bear the sheaves away?"
Loud and long the Master calleth;
    Rich reward He offers thee.
Who will answer, gladly saying,
    "Here am I, send me, send me"?

If you cannot speak like angels,
    If you cannot preach like Paul,
You can tell the love of Jesus,
    You can say He died for all.
If you cannot rouse the wicked
    With the judgment's dread alarms,
You can lead the little children
    To the Savior's waiting arms.

If you cannot be a watchman,
    Standing high on Zion's wall,
Pointing out the path to heaven,
    Off'ring life and peace to all,

With your prayers and with your bounties
　　You can do what God commands;
You can be like faithful Aaron,
　　Holding up the prophet's hands.

Let none hear you idly saying,
　　"There is nothing I can do,"
While the multitudes are dying
　　And the Master calls for you.
Take the task He gives you gladly,
　　Let His work your pleasure be;
Answer quickly when He calleth,
　　"Here am I, send me, send me!"
(LSB 826)

Shepherd of Tender Youth

Shepherd of tender youth,
Guiding in love and truth
　　Through devious ways;
Christ, our triumphant king,
We come Your name to sing
And here our children bring
　　To join Your praise.

You are the holy Lord,
O all-subduing Word,
   Healer of strife.
Yourself You did abase
That from sin's deep disgrace
You so might save our race
   And give us life.

You are the great High Priest;
You have prepared the feast
   Of holy love;
And in our mortal pain
None calls on You in vain;
Our plea do not disdain;
   Help from above.

O ever be our guide,
Our shepherd, and our pride,
   Our staff and song.
Jesus, O Christ of God,
By Your enduring Word
Lead us where You have trod;
   Make our faith strong.

So now, and till we die,
Sound we Your praises high
    And joyful sing:
Infants and all the throng,
Who to the Church belong,
Unite to swell the song
    To Christ, our king!

(*LSB* 864)

Let Children Hear the Mighty Deeds

Let children hear the mighty deeds
    Which God performed of old,
Which in our younger days we saw,
    And which our parents told.

So make to them His glories known,
    His works of pow'r and grace;
And we'll convey His wonders down
    Through ev'ry rising race.

Our sons and daughters we shall tell
    And they again to theirs
That generations yet unborn
    May teach them to their heirs.

O teach them with all diligence
  The truths of God's own Word,
To place in Him their confidence,
  To fear and trust their Lord,

To learn that in our God alone
  Their hope securely stands,
That they may never doubt His love
  But walk in His commands.

(*LSB* 867; st. 4 © 1941 CPH)

Go, My Children, with My Blessing

Go, My children, with My blessing,
  Never alone.
Waking, sleeping, I am with you;
  You are My own.
  In My love's baptismal river
  I have made you Mine forever.
Go, My children, with My blessing—
  You are My own.

Go, My children, sins forgiven,
  At peace and pure.

Here you learned how much I love you,
    What I can cure.
  Here you heard My dear Son's story;
  Here you touched Him, saw His glory.
Go, My children, sins forgiven,
    At peace and pure.

Go, My children, fed and nourished,
    Closer to Me;
Grow in love and love by serving,
    Joyful and free.
  Here My Spirit's power filled you;
  Here His tender comfort stilled you.
Go, My children, fed and nourished,
    Joyful and free.

I the Lord will bless and keep you
    And give you peace;
I the Lord will smile upon you
    And give you peace:
  I the Lord will be your Father,
  Savior, Comforter, and Brother.
Go, My children; I will keep you
    And give you peace.

(*LSB* 922; text by Jaroslav J. Vajda © 1983 CPH)

All You Works of God, Bless the Lord

All you works of God, bless the Lord!
All you angels, now bless the Lord;
Come, you heavens and pow'rs that be,
Praise the Lord and His majesty:

Refrain: Raise your voices high, praise and
magnify,
All you works of God, bless the Lord!
Raise your voices high, praise and magnify,
All you works of God, bless the Lord!

Sing, you sun and you moon above,
Stars of heaven, now sing His love;
Dew and showers, you winds that blow,
Heat and fire, you ice and snow: *Refrain*

Frost of winter with song so cold,
Dews of summer, your song unfold;
Light and darkness, you day and night,
Clouds of thunder, you lightnings bright:
Refrain

Hills and mountains, now sing His worth,
All you green things that grow on earth;
Seas and rivers, you springs and wells,
Beasts and cattle, you birds and whales:
Refrain

Come, humanity, sing along,
Sing, you people of God, a song;
Priests and servants, your Lord now bless,
Join, you spirits and souls at rest: *Refrain*

Bless the Lord, all you pure of heart;
All you humble, His praise impart;
God the Father and Son adore,
Bless the Spirit forevermore! *Refrain*

(*LSB* 930; text: © 1995 Stephen P. Starke, CPH)

Our Father Who Art in Heaven—IIa

Refrain: Our Father who art in heaven,
Thy name be hallowed,
Thy name be hallowed,
Heavenly Father.

May Thy kingdom come to us, O Lord;
May Thy holy will be done, O Lord;
As in heaven so on earth may Thy holy
will be done, O Lord. *Refrain*

Give us this day, O Lord, our daily bread;
Lord, forgive our trespasses, we pray,
As we forgive all those who trespass
against us, Lord. *Refrain*

Lead us not into temptation, Lord,
Lead us not into temptation, Lord,
But deliver us from evil, Lord, deliver us
from evil. *Refrain*

(*LSB* 958; © 2006 CPH)

By Your Life, O Lord, We Live

By Your life, O Lord, we live.
With Your Word, You now forgive.
By Your Spirit, we believe
That our Father gives reprieve.
Burdens bearing, home preparing, Jesus
gives us hope to sing;
Happy versing, we're rehearsing for our
King, for our King!

In the water, in the Word,
In the promise, be assured
Of His gift of grace so free,
Of the life eternally!
Through the Savior, given favor from the
Father on the throne
By the Spirit, let all hear it: Christ alone!
Christ alone!

In His death, we die to sin;
By His life, we live again.
Now with freedom all our days,
Tell the wonder of His ways!
Sister, brother, father, mother, caring

teacher, loving friend:
In all stations, all vocations, praises
send—never end!

Recommended tune: "Thine the Amen, Thine the Praise" (*LSB* 680)
© 2013 CPH

Humbly, Our Lord Jesus Labored

Humbly, our Lord Jesus labored,
Working calloused hands and feet.
Undertaking tasks less favored
Till His duty was complete.
Calling out to sin-sick masses,
Reaching out with healing love.
Breath through dying lips, He passes
Promises of life above.

Come, disciples, let us hurry,
Sharing love both far and wide.
Guard against our doubt and worry;
Holy Spirit, be our Guide.
May we never tire of serving
As our Savior loved us true.
Keep our idle hearts from swerving
From what God would have us do.

As we wait for Christ's returning,
Let us gladly work for good.
May He never find us spurning
Any task of servanthood.
We are loved and free to praise Him
With our hands, our feet, our voice.
With our bodies, whole and risen,
May we evermore rejoice!

Recommended tune: "Jesus, Refuge of the Weary" (*LSB* 423)
© 2013 CPH

Loving Father, Guide Your Children

Loving Father, guide Your children:
Raising offspring of our own.
Do not keep Your good will hidden;
By Your Word, let it be shown.
Your unfailing love and favor
Strengthens us to love anew.
Your good gifts we gladly savor,
Sharing all we have from You.

Lord, You called out to the smallest
With Your open, waiting arms.
Shield against what may befall us;

Keep Your loved ones from all harm.
Give protection to the lowly,
Courage to the weak of heart,
Wisdom to Your children holy,
Voice to share what You impart.

Help us, Lord, to share Your teaching
To the young from age to age.
Your Good News to all ends reaching,
Let us pass Your sacred page.
We remember Your sweet promise
That our joy will never end.
Though our earthly breath pass from us,
We will reunite again!

With our eyes firm on the future,
And the hope of "evermore,"
We will share words from our Teacher
As were taught to us before.
As we train each son and daughter
And the Church grows every day,
We proclaim that Jesus bought Her,
Washing all Her sins away.

Recommended tune: "Come, Thou Fount of Every Blessing" (*LSB* 686)
© 2014 CPH.